SQL and PL/SQL in Practice

Volume1: Learning the Basics in No Time

Djoni Darmawikarta

Table of Contents

Preface 1

SQL and PL/SQL 1

Using this book 1

Prerequisite 1

Book Examples 2

Part I: SQL... 3

Chapter 1: Data is Table 5

Creating a Table 5

Adding Rows 6

Updating Data 10

Deleting Data 11

Altering Table 12

Removing Table 12

Chapter 2: Basic Queries... 13

Filtering Rows 14

Comparison Operators 15

Compound Condition... 15

Negating Operator... 16

Comparing to a List of Values.. 17

Imprecise Comparison... 18

Handling NULL... 18

Column Alias.. 19

Limiting Number of Output Rows 20

DISTINCT 21

Aggregate Functions.. 22

The CASE expression 23

    Simple CASE 23

    Searched CASE 24

Ordering Output Rows 26

    Ordering by One Column 27

    Direction of Order 28

    Ordering by Multiple Columns 28

    Different Directions on Different Columns 29

    ORDER after WHERE 30

Chapter 3: Grouping 31

  The GROUP BY Clause 31

    GROUP BY Multiple Columns 32

  The HAVING Clause 33

Chapter 4: Joins 37

  Querying Multiple Tables 37

  Using Table Aliases 38

  Joining More than Two Tables 39

Chapter 5: Subqueries 41

  Single-Row Subqueries 41

  Multiple-Row Subqueries 41

  Correlated Subqueries 43

Chapter 6: Compound Queries 45

  UNION ALL 45

  UNION 46

  INTERSECT 47

  MINUS 48

Chapter 7: Built-in Functions 51

  Numeric Functions 51

ABS 51

ROUND 51

SIGN 53

Character Functions 53

CONCAT 53

LOWER and UPPER 54

LENGTH 54

SUBSTR 55

Datetime Functions 55

CURRENT_DATE 56

TO_CHAR 56

NULL-related functions 57

COALESCE 57

NULLIF 58

NVL 59

Part II: PL/SQL 61

Chapter 8: Block 63

Declaration Part 63

Executable Part 65

Exception-handling Part 66

Block Nesting 68

Block Label 69

Variable Visibility 70

Same-Name Variables 72

Comment 73

Chapter 9: Variable Declaration 75

Data Type... 75

Other Data Types 75

Assignment Operator 76

Initial Value.. 76

NOT NULL 78

Constant 79

Chapter 10: Executable Statement 81

Assignment, Computation, and Calling Procedure................... 81

Control Statements 82

   IF THEN ELSE 82

   IF THEN ELSIF.. 85

LOOP.. 87

   Nested LOOP 88

   Fixed Number of Iteration.. 89

   WHILE Loop.. 90

CASE.. 92

   Simple CASE.. 92

   Searched CASE 93

Chapter 11: Exception-handling.. 95

Multiple Exception-handlers... 96

Combining Exceptions 96

Visibility of Exception 97

Predefined Exceptions 99

SQLCODE and SQLERRM functions... 100

Defining Oracle Error... 100

User Defined Exception 101

Part III SQL and PL/SQL together 103

Chapter 12: Using SQL in PL/SQL.. 105

PL/SQL Advantage over SQL's 105

INTO clause 106

Only One Row 106

ROWTYPE and TYPE 107

SELECT for UPDATE 108

Commit and Rollback 109

Transaction 110

    Savepoint 111

    Multiple Transactions 112

DDL (Data Definition Language) 112

Chapter 13: Cursor 115

Cursor Parameters 116

PL/SQL Variable in the Query 117

Cursor Last Row 118

Cursor Attributes 119

Cursor FOR Loop 121

Cursor FOR LOOP short cut 122

Chapter 14: Subprogram 123

Function 123

Procedure 125

Stored Programs 126

Package 128

    Creating Package 128

Trigger 130

    Conditioning the Trigger 131

Appendix A: Setting Up 133

Installing Database Express Edition 133

Installing SQL Developer 136

Creating Connection 139

Creating Database Account.. 141

Creating Your Connection 144

Showing Line Numbers 146

Deleting the *system* Connection.. 148

Appendix B: Using SQL Developer 151

Entering SQL statement and PL/SQL source code 151

SQL Statement 152

Inserting Rows 153

PL/SQL program 154

Multiple worksheets for a connection 155

Storing the source code.. 157

Opening a source code 158

Storing the listings in Appendix A into files 159

Running SQL or PL/SQL from a file 159

Clearing a Worksheet 160

Displaying Output 160

Clearing Dbms Output 164

Index 167

Preface

Learn the Basics in No Time, the first volume of the *SQL and PL/SQL in Practice* series, is for Oracle database programmers.

If you have no prior or limited skill of SQL and PL/SQL, and you want to learn to use the two individually or together, then this book is perfect for you.

SQL and PL/SQL

SQL (Structured Query Language) is the standard database language. PL/SQL (Procedural Language/SQL) is the procedural language extension of SQL. PL/SQL is integrated within the Oracle database. When you install an Oracle database, PL/SQL is included in the installation.

A PL/SQL program can have *both* SQL statements and procedural statements. In the program, the SQL statements are used to manipulate *sets* of data stored in a database, while the procedural statements are used to process *individual* piece of data and control the program flow by, for example, using the if-then-else and looping structures.

Using this book

The book has three parts. In Part I you will learn: how to store and maintain SQL data and to query the data; in Part II, the parts of a PL/SQL program and how to use if-then and loop control structures; and in Part III, how to embed, control the flow of SQL statements and process the rows returned by SQL query, within PL/SQL program.

The major topics covered in the book are listed in the Table of Contents.

When you finish reading the book and trying its examples, you would have equipped yourself with SQL and PL/SQL fundamental skills.

Prerequisite

You don't need to have any SQL and PL/SQL skills to successfully use this book.

Book Examples

To learn the most out of this book, try the book examples. Set up your own Oracle database and SQL Developer tool to freely and safely try the examples.

You can download free of charge both the database and the tool from the Oracle website. Appendix A is your guide to install the software; Appendix B shows you how to particularly use SQL Developer to try the book examples.

The examples were tested on Oracle Database 11g Express Edition release 2 and SQL Developer version 4.

Part I: SQL

In this part you will learn the basics of SQL: how to create table, add and maintain data in the tables, and write queries.

Chapter 1: Data is Table

SQL data is stored as tables. When you add a record of data, the record is stored as a row of the table. Row has columns.

Data about product, its code, name, price, and launch date, for example, can be stored as a table with four columns. Table and its columns must be named.

The following four rows are sample of the product table.

P_CODE	P_NAME	PRICE	LAUNCH_DT
1 1	Nail	10	16-03-31
2 2	Washer	15	16-03-29
3 3	Nut	15	16-03-29
4 4	Screw	20	16-03-30

PRODUCT — Columns **Data** Model | Constraints | Grants | Statistics | Triggers — Sort.. Filter:

Creating a Table

Before you add rows, its table must first be defined (created in the database) by executing a *CREATE TABLE* statement with the following syntax.

```
CREATE TABLE table_name
   (column_name data_type,
    column_name data_type,
    ...
    PRIMARY KEY (columns));
```

The CREATE TABLE statement in Example 1-1 will create our product table. When you run the statement successfully, the message on the Script Output pane will confirm that the table has been created.

```
djoni
▷ 🗐 🗐 ▾ 🗐 🗐  🗐 🗐  🗐 🗐 🗐 🗐 🗐

Worksheet   Query Builder
  1 ⊟CREATE TABLE product
  2  ┊   (
  3  ┊       p_code VARCHAR2(6), p_name VARCHAR2(15),
  4  ┊       price  NUMBER(4,2), launch_dt DATE,
  5  ┊       PRIMARY KEY (p_code)
  6  ┊   );
  7  ┊

▲▼
🗐 Script Output ×
📌 🗐 🗐 🗐 🗐   Task completed in 0.075 seconds
Table PRODUCT created.
```

Example 1-1 Creating table

A column must have a *data types*. The data types we use for our product table are:

VARCHAR2(6), which specifies a variable length string up to 6 characters.

NUMBER(4,2), a numeric with two decimals from -99.99 to +99.99.

DATE, a date for storing date

To uniquely identify an individual product row, we designate the p_code column as the *primary key* of the table.

Adding Rows

Once the CREATE TABLE statement is successfully executed, rows of product data can be added using the INSERT statement.

```
INSERT INTO table
   (column_1, column_2,... )
VALUES (value_1, value_2,... ));
```

Let's insert the first row as shown Example 1-2 below. The Script Output confirms the row has been inserted.

Example 1-2 Inserting a row

If you get an error message caused by a wrong date format, execute the following statement, and then re-execute the INSERT statement.

```
ALTER SESSION
SET NLS_DATE_FORMAT = 'DD-MON_YYYY';
```

To see the row, run the Example 1-3 query. The row will be shown on the Query Result pane.

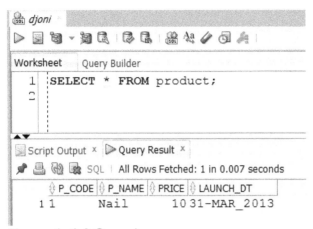

Example 1-3 Querying row

You can only add one row in an INSERT statement. To add five rows, for example, you need five INSERT statements (Example 1-4). Run the five statements by pressing F5. You should see five confirmation messages.

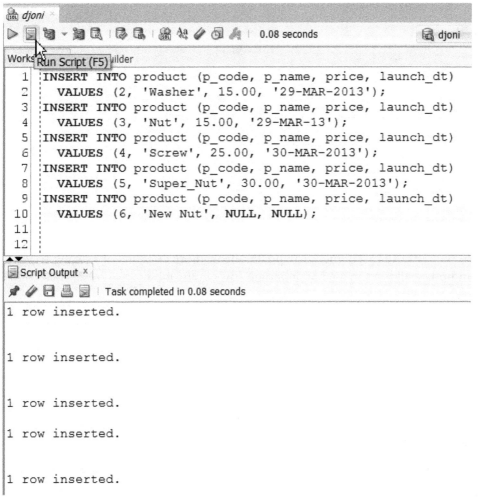

Example 1-4 Inserting five rows

Now issue a COMMIT command to persist (confirm the storage of) the rows (Example 1-5). You should see the "Commit complete" message on the Script Output pane.

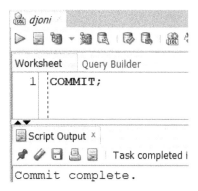

Example 1-5 Committing inserted rows

Updating Data

You use the UPDATE statement to update one or more columns of existing rows. You can update all rows in a table or certain rows in the table.

The syntax for the UPDATE statement is as follows

```
UPDATE table_name
SET column_1 = new_value_1 [,
    column_2 = new_value_2,
    ... ]
[WHERE condition];
```

The statement in Example 1-6 below will update the price of product with p_code = 5. Without the WHERE clause all products will have their prices updated.

Example 1-6 Updating row

Deleting Data

To delete a row or multiple rows in a table, use the DELETE statement. You can specify which rows to be deleted by using the WHERE clause.

The syntax for the DELETE statement is as follows

```
DELETE FROM table
[WHERE condition];
```

The Example 1-7 statement below deletes products except 'Nut'.

Example 1-7 Deleting row

You can issue a ROLLBACK command to return the data values back to before the deletion as seen in the following Example 1-8.

Example 1-8 Rolling back deletion

Altering Table

Use the ALTER TABLE statement to rename a table, rename or changing its column using the ALTER TABLE statement.

The following statements rename the old_product table, rename p_name column of the new older_product table, change the price column size, then remove the launch_dt column and the last one adds the launch_dt column back.

```
ALTER ALTER TABLE old_product RENAME TO older_product;
ALTER TABLE older_product RENAME COLUMN p_name TO prod_nam;
ALTER TABLE older_product MODIFY price NUMBER(6,2);
ALTER TABLE older_product DROP COLUMN launch_dt;
ALTER TABLE older_product ADD launch_dt DATE;
```

Removing Table

A DROP TABLE statement removes the table and all its data.

```
DROP TABLE table_name;
```

Chapter 2: Basic Queries

To query (read) SQL data, use the SELECT statement with the following syntax.

`SELECT column_names FROM table_name [WHERE condition];`

Only the SELECT and FROM clauses are mandatory. The optional WHERE clause filters the rows; only rows that satisfy the condition will be in the query result (output). If your query does not have a WHERE clause, the result will be all rows of the table.

In the SELECT clause you list the output columns in the order you want as demonstrated in Example 2-1.

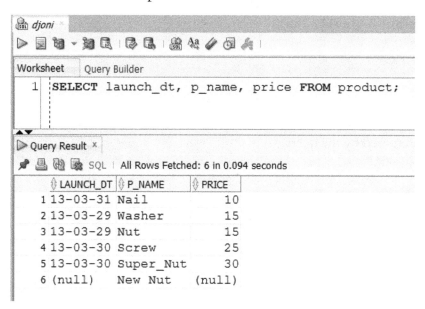

Example 2-1 SELECT statement

Note: Specify * if you want to query all columns and do not care about the order of the output columns (Example 2-2). The output columns will be in the order defined in their CREATE TABLE statement.

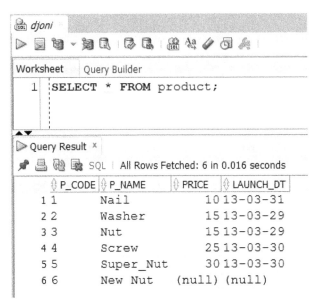

Example 2-2 SELECT *

Filtering Rows

Use the WHERE clause to select specific rows. In Example 2-3 only rows whose price is 15 will be returned by the query.

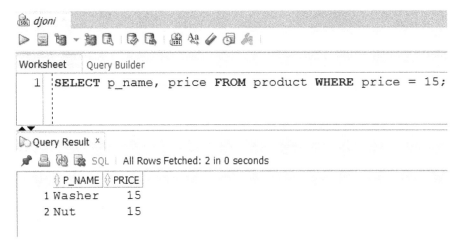

Example 2-3 Selecting on price

Comparison Operators

You can use other comparison operators in addition to the equal sign (=)

Operator	Description
=	Equal to
<	Less than
>	Greater than
<=	Less than or equal to
>=	Greater than or equal to
!=	Not equal to

The following query (Example 2-4) returns only rows whose p_name is not Nut.

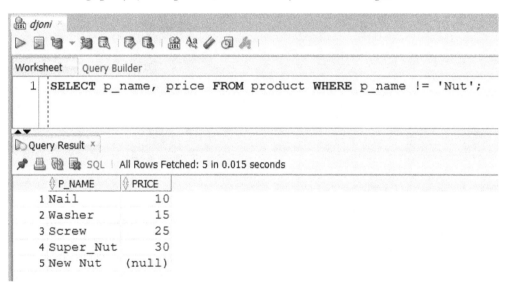

Example 2-4 Comparison operator !=

Compound Condition

Using OR and AND, you can form a more complex condition involving more than one comparison operator.

In Example 2-5 query the result of the condition (launch_dt >= '30-MAR-13' OR price > 15) is true for Nail, Screw and Super_Nut rows in the product table; AND-ing this result with the (p_name != 'Nail') predicate results in two products, the Screw and Super_Nut.

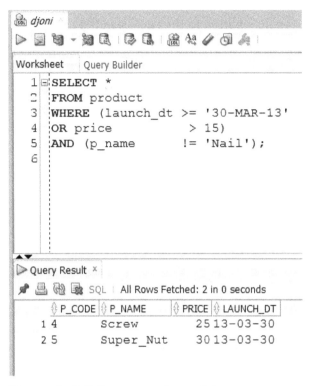

Example 2-5 Compound condition

Note that New Nut does not satisfy the condition because applying any of the comparison operators to NULL results in false (the price and launch_dt of the New Nut are NULL). The section "Handling NULL" later in this chapter explains more about NULL.

Negating Operator

Use NOT to negate a condition and return rows that do not satisfy the condition. The query in Example 2-6 negates the condition of the previous query, returning the two rows not returned by that previous query.

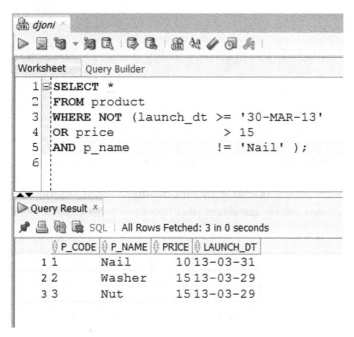

Example 2-6 NOT operator

Comparing to a List of Values

Use an IN operator to compare a column to a list of values as shown in Example 2-7 below.

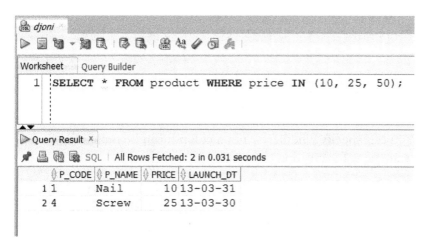

Example 2-7 NOT operator

Imprecise Comparison

The LIKE operator allows you to specify an imprecise equality condition. The syntax is as follows.

```
SELECT columns FROM table
WHERE column LIKE ' ... wildcard_character ... ';
```

The wildcard character can be a percentage sign (%) to represent any number of characters or an underscore (_) to represent a single occurrence of any character.

The query in Example 2-8 uses the LIKE operator to find products whose name starts with N and is followed by two other characters plus products whose name starts with Sc and can be of any length.

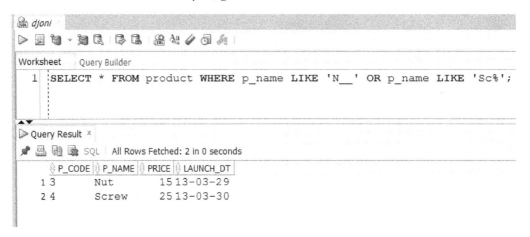

Example 2-8 LIKE operator

Handling NULL

NULL, an SQL reserved word, represents the absence of data. NULL is applicable to any data type. It is not the same as a numeric zero or an empty string or a 0000/00/00 date. You can specify whether or not a column can be null in the CREATE TABLE statement for creating the table.

The result of applying any of the comparison operators on NULL is always NULL. You can only test whether or not a column is NULL by using the IS NULL (Example 2-9 below) or IS NOT NULL operator.

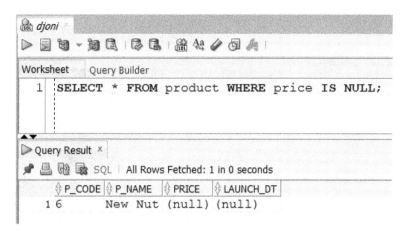

Example 2-9 is NULL

Column Alias

By default the names of the output columns in the query output are the names of the columns of the queried table. However, you don't have to be stuck with the original column names. You can give them different names or aliases if you wish.

The syntax for the SELECT clause that uses aliases is as follows.

```
SELECT column_1 AS alias1, column_2 AS alias2, ...
FROM table;
```

An alias can consist of one or multiple words. You must enclose a multiword alias with quotes, e.g. "PRODUCT NAME".

The output columns do not need to be columns from the table. It can be string or numeric expressions that include string or numeric literals, operators, and functions.

Example 2-10 below is an example.

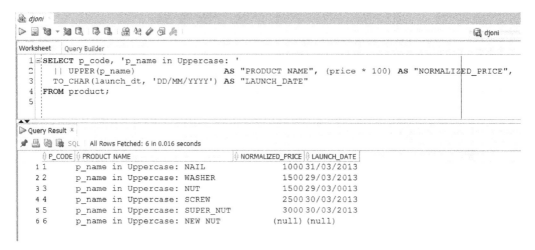

Example 2-10 Column alias

The output of the query will have four columns. The first output column, p_code, is a column from the product table.

The second output column (aliased "PRODUCT NAME") is an expression that contains three parts, a literal 'p_name in Uppercase: ', a concatenation string operator (||), and UPPER(p_name). The latter, UPPER, is a function applied to the p_name column from the product table. The UPPER function changes the case of the product names to uppercase.

The third output column ("NORMALIZED_PRICE") is an arithmetic expression (price*100).

The last output column ("LAUNCH_DATE") is the launch_date column formatted as DD/MM/YYYY.

You can use other arithmetic operators in addition to the multiplication (*) operator in your column. These include addition (+), subtraction (-), and division (/)

Limiting Number of Output Rows

You can limit the number of output row by using the ROWNUM pseudo column. Its syntax is as follows.

```
SELECT columns FROM table(s)
WHERE conditions AND ROWNUM < count;
```

The maximum number of output rows of a query that employs ROWNUM will be *count* – 1.

Example 2-11 demonstrates the use of ROWNUM.

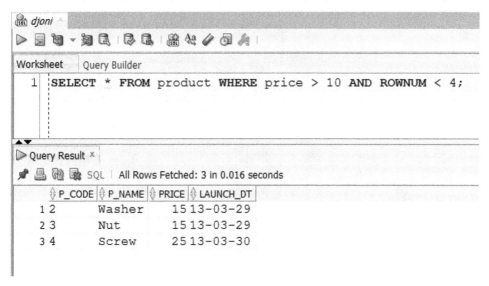

Example 2-11 Using ROWNUM

Without the expression ROWNUM < 4, the number of output rows would be 4.

DISTINCT

A query may return duplicate rows. Two rows are duplicates if each of their columns contains exactly the same data. If you don't want to see duplicate output rows, use DISTINCT in your SELECT clause. You can use DISTINCT on one column or multiple columns (see Example 2-12 next).

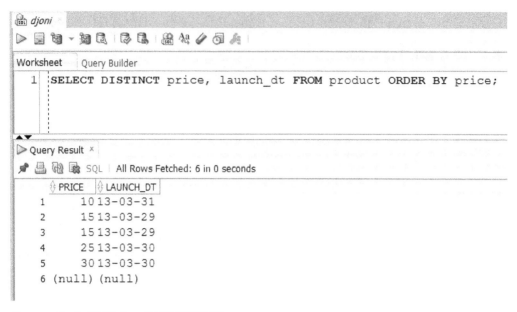

Example 2-12 Using DISTINCT

Aggregate Functions

You can manipulate your query output further by using aggregate functions. Here are the aggregate functions.

Function	Description
MAX(column)	The maximum column value
MIN(column)	The minimum column value
SUM(column)	The sum of column values
AVG(column)	The average column value
COUNT(column)	The count of rows
COUNT(*)	The count of all rows including NULL.

Example 2-13 is an example query. Note that while COUNT(PRICE) only counts price that is not null, COUNT(*) takes into account all prices including NULL.

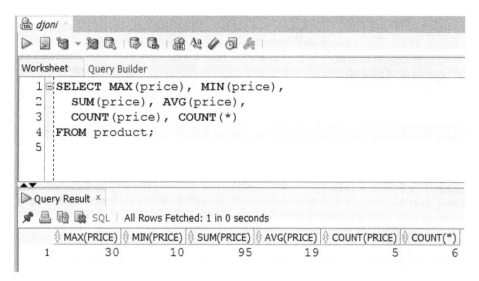

Example 2-13 Aggregate functions

The CASE expression

CASE allows you to have a logic on an output column. CASE comes in two flavors: Simple and Searched.

Simple CASE

The general syntax for the Simple CASE is as follows.

```
SELECT columns,
  CASE column_name
    WHEN equal_value1
    THEN output_value1
    WHEN equal_value2
    THEN output_value2
    WHEN ...
    [ELSE else_value]
  END AS output_column
FROM table
WHERE ... ;
```

In the Simple CASE, the value of *column_name* is compared to *equal_value*, starting from the first WHEN and down to the last WHEN. When a *column_name* value matches its *equal_value*, its *output_value* is the value of the *output_column*, and the rest of then WHEN is not evaluated (the CASE process stops).

If no *column_name* matches its *equal_values*, *else_value* is then the value of the output_column. If you do not provide else, the output_column is NULL.

The following query (Example 2-14) uses a Simple CASE expression for the price column to produce a price_cat (price category) output column.

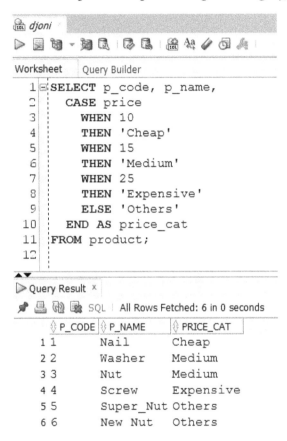

Example 2-14 Simple CASE

Searched CASE

The case in the Simple CASE compares a column with various values. On the hand, the case in the Searched CASE can be any condition. Here is the syntax for the Searched CASE.

```
SELECT columns,
```

```
CASE
   WHEN condition1
   THEN output_value1
   WHEN condition2
   THEN output_value2
   WHEN ...
   ELSE else_value
   END AS output_column
FROM table
WHERE ... ;
```

The conditions are evaluated starting from the first WHEN and down to the last WHEN. If a WHEN condition is met, its THEN output_value is returned to the output_column and the CASE process stops. If none of the WHEN conditions is met, *else_value* is returned if there exists an ELSE clause. If no condition is met and no ELSE clause exists, NULL will be returned.

The following query uses a Searched CASE. While the Simple CASE in Example 2-14 categorized the products based on only their prices, the Searched CASE in Example 2-15 categorizes the products based on the various conditions which can involve more than just the price. Note that in the Search CASE, NULL equality can be a condition, something that is not allowed in the Simple CASE.

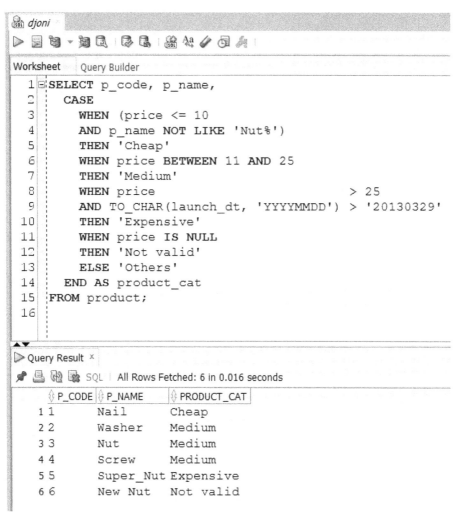

Example 2-15 Searched CASE

Ordering Output Rows

To provide better visualization of the output, you can order output rows based on certain criteria. To order the output, use the ORDER BY clause. The ORDER BY clause must appear last in a SELECT statement.

Here is the syntax for a query having the ORDER BY clause.

```
SELECT columns
FROM table
WHERE condition ORDER BY column(s)
```

You can order output rows in one of the following methods.

- by one or more columns
- in ascending or descending direction
- by using the GROUP BY clause
- by using UNION and other set operators

Each of the methods is explained in the subsections below.

Ordering by One Column

To order your query output rows, use the ORDER BY clause with one column. For instance, have a look at Example 2-16.

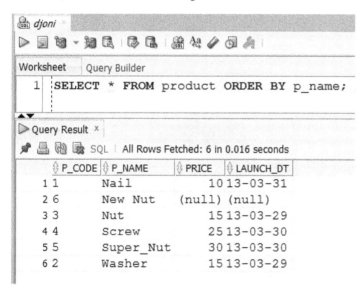

Example 2-16 Order by one column

Direction of Order

The default direction is ascending. To order a column in descending direction, use the DESC reserved word. The following query (Example 2-17) is similar to Example 2-16 except that the output is presented in descending order. The output rows will be returned with p_name sorted in descending order.

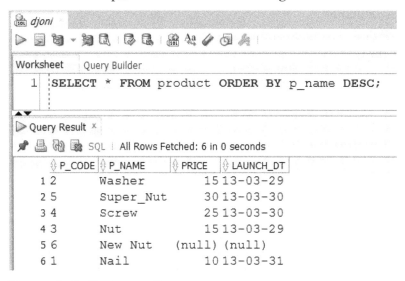

Example 2-17 Descending

Ordering by Multiple Columns

To order by more than one column, list the columns in the ORDER BY clause. The sequence of columns listed is significant. The order will be conducted by the first column in the list, followed by the second column, and so on. For example, if the ORDER BY clause has two columns, the query output will first be ordered by the first column. Any rows with identical values in the first column will be further ordered by the second column.

Example 2-18 uses an ORDER BY clause with two columns. The output rows will first be ordered by launch_dt and then by price, both in ascending order. The secondary ordering by price is seen on the Screw and Super_Nut rows. Their launch_dt's are the same, 30-MAR-13. Their prices are different, Screw's lower than Super_Nut's, hence Screw row comes before the Super_Nut.

Example 2-18 Multiple columns ordering

Different Directions on Different Columns

You can apply different order directions on ordered columns too. In Example 2-19, the query uses different directions on different columns in its ORDER BY clause.

Example 2-19 Different directions

ORDER after WHERE

If your SELECT statement has both the WHERE clause and the ORDER BY clause, ORDER BY must appear after the WHERE clause.

For example, the query in Example 2-20 has both WHERE and ORDER BY. This query will return only Nut products. If you execute the query, you will see one row only, the Nut, in the output window.

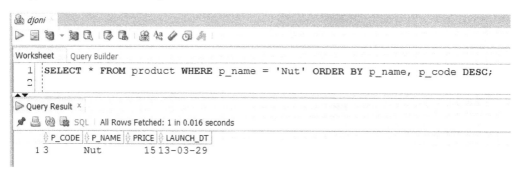

Example 2-19 Different directions

Chapter 3: Grouping

A group is a set of rows having the same value on specific columns. In Chapter 3, "Query Output" you learned how to apply aggregate functions on all output rows. In this chapter you learn how to create groups and apply aggregate functions on those groups.

The GROUP BY Clause

In a query the GROUP BY clause appears after the WHERE clause and before the ORDER clause, if any. Here is the syntax for a SELECT statement with the WHERE, GROUP BY, and ORDER BY clauses.

```
SELECT columns,
  aggregate_function(group_columns)
FROM table(s)
WHERE condition
GROUP BY group_columns
ORDER BY column(s);
```

As an example, the query in Example 3-1 groups the output from the product table by their launch date.

The query output will have four rows, one for each of the four grouped launch dates. Note that the COUNT(price) element, which counts the rows with a value on their price column, produces 0. On the other hand, the COUNT(*) element, which counts the NULL launch dates, produces 1.

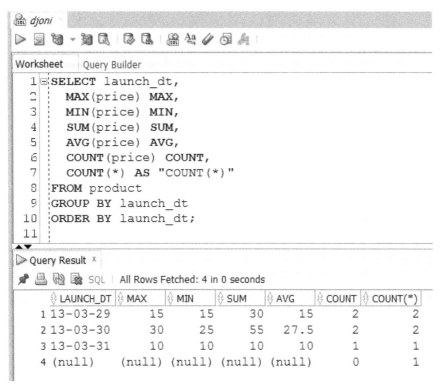

Example 3-1 GROUP BY

You can group by more than one column. If you do that, rows having the same value on all the columns will form a group. As an example, the query in Example 3-2 groups rows by price and launch date.

GROUP BY Multiple Columns

Look at Example 3-2. Even though the Screw and Super_Nut have the same price, they have different launch dates, and therefore form different groups.

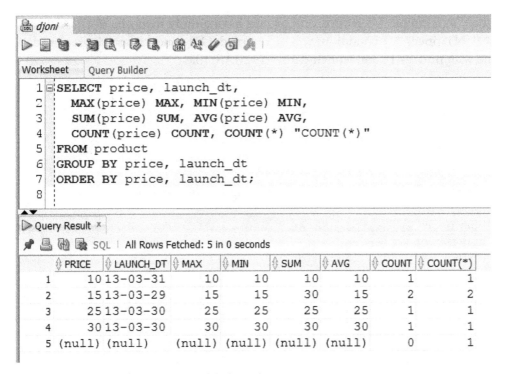

Example 3-2 GROUP BY multiple columns

The HAVING Clause

You use the WHERE condition to select individual **rows**. Use the HAVING condition to select individual **groups**. Only groups that satisfy the condition in the HAVING clause will be returned by the query. In other words, the HAVING condition is on the aggregate, not on a column.

If present, the HAVING clause must appear after the GROUP BY, as in the following syntax.

```
SELECT columns,
  aggregate_function(group_columns)
FROM table(s)
WHERE condition
GROUP BY group_columns
HAVING aggregate_condition
ORDER BY columns;
```

The query in Example 3-3 returns only groups having more than one row (satisfying the COUNT(price) > 1 condition) will be returned. Only one row will be returned, the one with price = 15 and launch date = 29-MAR-13.

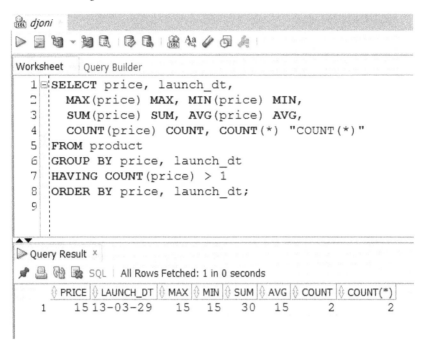

Example 3-3 HAVING

If a WHERE clause is present, it must appear after the GROUP BY clause. Individual rows will be selected by the WHERE condition first before grouping occurs. In the case of Example 3-4, Super_Nut does not satisfy the WHERE condition. As such, it is not included in the aggregation.

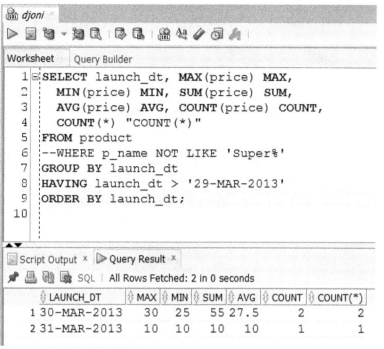

```
SELECT launch_dt, MAX(price) MAX,
  MIN(price) MIN, SUM(price) SUM,
  AVG(price) AVG, COUNT(price) COUNT,
  COUNT(*) "COUNT(*)"
FROM product
--WHERE p_name NOT LIKE 'Super%'
GROUP BY launch_dt
HAVING launch_dt > '29-MAR-2013'
ORDER BY launch_dt;
```

LAUNCH_DT	MAX	MIN	SUM	AVG	COUNT	COUNT(*)
1 30-MAR-2013	30	25	55	27.5	2	2
2 31-MAR-2013	10	10	10	10	1	1

Example 3-4 WHERE

Chapter 4: Joins

A real-world database typically has dozens or even hundreds of inter-related tables. A customer order table has the details of customer who ordered and product ordered in separate tables. A query to retrieve the details has to relate rows from the three tables.

Querying Multiple Tables

To query data from multiple tables, use the JOIN clause with the following syntax.

```
SELECT columns FROM table_1
JOIN table_2 ON column1 = column2 . . .
JOIN table_z ON column2 = columnz;
```

Assume, in addition to the product table, we have the following order and customer tables. Note that the c_order table has c_no and p_code columns, which we use to join to the customer and product table, respectively.

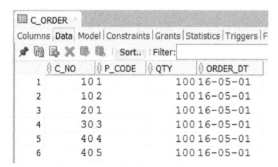

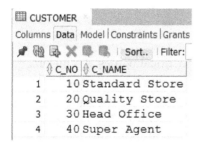

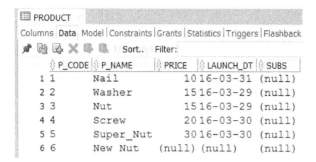

The following query (Example 4-1) returns the name of every customer who has placed one or more orders.

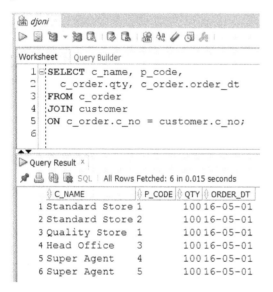

Example 4-1 JOIN

Using Table Aliases

In a join query, different tables can have columns with identical names. To make sure you refer to the correct column of a table, you need to qualify it with its table. In the previous example, c_order.c_no (the c_no column of the c_order table) and customer.c_no (the c_no column of the customer_table) were how the c_no columns were qualified. A table alias can be a more convenient (and shorter) way to qualify a column.

Example 4-2 is an example.

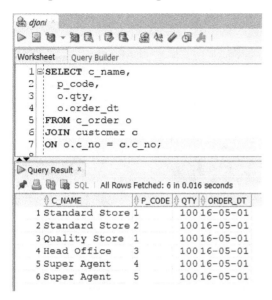

Example 4-2 Table alias

Joining More than Two Tables

Here is an example (Example 4-3) of joining three tables. This query returns the customer names and their orders.

Example 4-3 Multi tables join

You can also apply WHERE conditions for selecting rows on a join query. In Example 4-4 below, only products with names that do not start with "Super" will be returned by the following query.

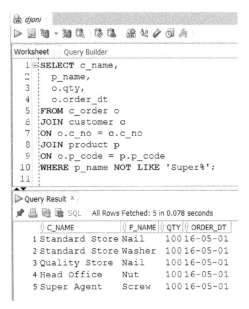

Example 4-4 WHERE condition

Chapter 5: Subqueries

A subquery is a query nested within another query. The containing query is called an outer query. A subquery in turn can have a nested query, making it a multiple nested query.

Single-Row Subqueries

A single-row subquery is a subquery that returns a single value. A single-row subquery can be placed in the WHERE clause of an outer query. The return value of the subquery is compared with a column of the outer query using one of the comparison operators.

The outer query in Example 5-1 returns all products from the product table with highest price as returned by the subquery.

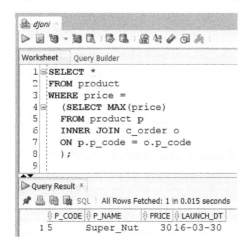

Example 5-1 Single row subquery

Multiple-Row Subqueries

A subquery that returns more than one value is called a multiple-row subquery. This type of subquery also occurs in the WHERE clause of an outer query, however instead of using a comparison operator, you use IN or NOT IN in the WHERE clause.

Example 5-2 is an example.

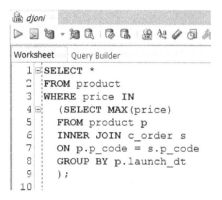

Example 5-2 Multi rows subquery

The grouping subquery returns three maximum prices:

Hence, the overall query returns products that have those maximum prices.

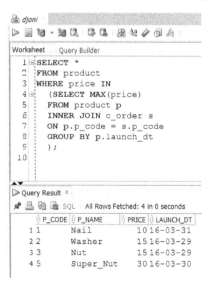

Correlated Subqueries

All the preceding subqueries are independent of their outer queries. A subquery can also be related to its outer query, where one or more column from the outer query table is (are) related to the column(s) of the subquery table in the WHERE clause of the subquery. This type of subquery is called the correlated subquery.

The query in Example 5-3 contains a correlated subquery that returns only customers who have not ordered any product whose name contains 'Nut'. Note that the c_no column of the outer query table, customer, is related to the c_no column of the c_order table of the subquery.

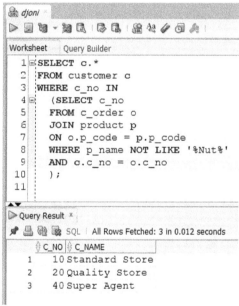

Example 5-3 Correlated subquery

Chapter 6: Compound Queries

You can combine the results of two or more SELECT statements using the UNION ALL, UNION, INTERSECT, or MINUS operators. The number of output columns from every statement must be the same and the corresponding columns must have identical or compatible data types.

UNION ALL

When you combine two or more queries with the UNION ALL operator, the overall output will be the total rows from all the queries as demonstrated in the following example (Example 6-1) with two SELECT statements.

Note that the 'FIRST QUERY' and 'SECOND_QUERY' literals are just labels to identify which of the queries the row comes from.

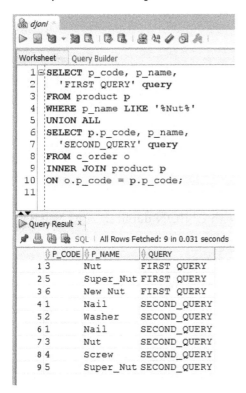

Example 6-1 UNION ALL

Note that the output of the preceding query comprises all the records form the first SELECT statement followed by the rows from the second SELECT statement. You can order the results as you want using an ORDER clause, as demonstrated in Example 6-2 next.

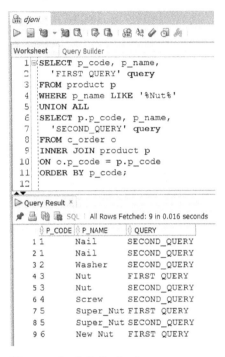

Example 6-2 Ordering

UNION

UNION is similar to UNION ALL. However, with UNION duplicate rows will be returned once only.

Look at Example 6-3 below.

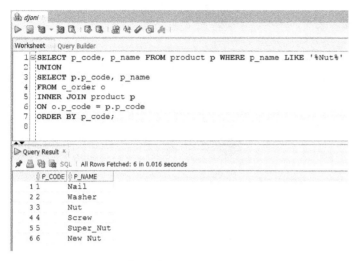

Example 6-3 UNION ALL

INTERSECT

When you combine two or more queries with the INTERSECT operator, the output will consist of rows common to all the participating SELECT statements. In other words, only if a row is returned by all the SELECT statements will the row be included in the final result.

Example 6-4 demonstrates the use of INTERSETCT.

```
djoni
Worksheet    Query Builder
 1 ⊟SELECT p_code, p_name FROM product p WHERE p_name LIKE '%Nut%'
 2  INTERSECT
 3  SELECT p.p_code, p_name
 4  FROM c_order o
 5  INNER JOIN product p
 6  ON o.p_code = p.p_code
 7  ORDER BY p_code;
 8

Query Result ×
    SQL   All Rows Fetched: 2 in 0 seconds
     P_CODE  P_NAME
 1 3         Nut
 2 5         Super_Nut
```

Example 6-4 INTERSECT

MINUS

When you combine two SELECT statements using the MINUS operator, the final output will be rows from the first query that are not returned by the second query, as show in Example 6-5.

```
djoni
Worksheet    Query Builder
 1 ⊟SELECT p_code, p_name FROM product p WHERE p_name LIKE '%Nut%'
 2  MINUS
 3  SELECT p.p_code, p_name
 4  FROM c_order o
 5  INNER JOIN product p
 6  ON o.p_code = p.p_code
 7  ORDER BY p_code;
 8

Query Result ×
    SQL   All Rows Fetched: 1 in 0 seconds
     P_CODE  P_NAME
 1 6         New Nut
```

Example 6-5 MINUS

With MINUS, the order of constituting SELECT statements is important. If you swap the two SELECT statements in the preceding query, the output will be totally different, as seen in Example 6-6.

```
5  ON o.p_code = p.p_code
6  MINUS
7  SELECT p_code,
8      p_name
9  FROM product p
10 WHERE p_name LIKE '%Nut%'
11 ORDER BY p_code;
12
13
```

Query Result ×

SQL | All Rows Fetched: 3 in 0 secon

	P_CODE	P_NAME
1	1	Nail
2	2	Washer
3	4	Screw

Example 6-6 SELECT order

Chapter 7: Built-in Functions

The Oracle database provides functions that you can use in your queries. These built-in functions can be grouped into numeric functions, character functions, datetime functions, and functions for handling null values. This chapter introduces some of these functions.

Numeric Functions

The following are some of the more important numeric functions.

ABS

ABS(n) returns the absolute value of n.

The following query returns the absolute value of (price - 20.00) as the third column.

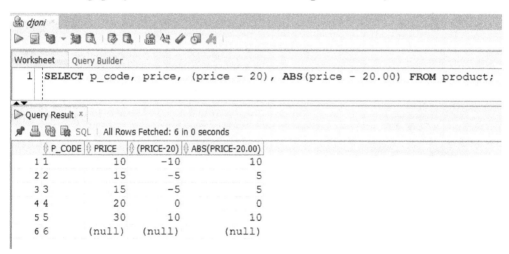

ROUND

ROUND(n, d) returns a number rounded to a certain number of decimal places. The argument n is the number to be rounded and d the number of decimal places.

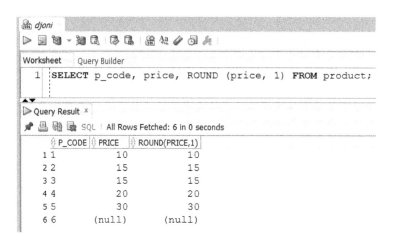

SIGN

SIGN(n) returns a value indicating the sign of n. This function returns -1 for $n < 0$, 0 for $n = 0$, and 1 for $n > 0$. As an example, the following query uses SIGN to return the sign of (price − 15).

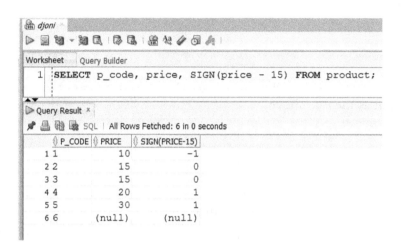

Character Functions

The following are some of the more important string functions.

CONCAT

CONCAT(*string1*, *string2*) concatenates *string1* and *string2* and returns the result. If you pass a number as an argument, the number will first be converted to a string. In the following example three strings, *p_name*, a dash, and *description*, are concatenated.

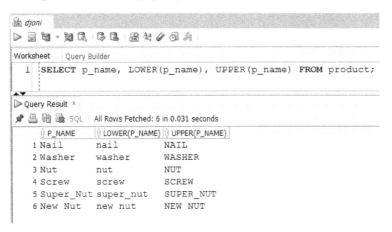

You can also use the || operator to concatenate strings. The following query produces the same output as the one above.

```
SELECT p_code, p_name || ' -- ' || price FROM product;
```

LOWER and UPPER

LOWER(*str*) converts *str* to lowercase and UPPER(*str*) converts *str* to uppercase. For example, the following query uses LOWER and UPPER.

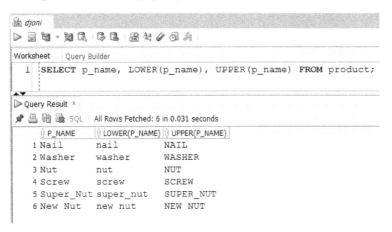

LENGTH

LENGTH(*str*) returns the length of string *str*. The length of a string is the number of characters in it. For example, the following query returns the length of p_name as the second column.

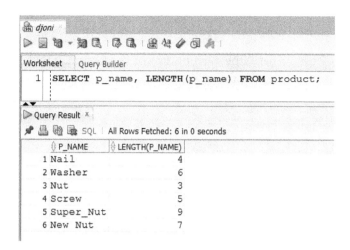

SUBSTR

SUBSTR(*str*, *start_position*, [*length*]) returns a substring of *str* starting from the position indicated by *start_position*. If *length* is not specified, the function returns a substring from *start_position* to the last character in *str*. If *length* is present, the function returns a substring which is *length* characters long starting from *start_position*. If *length* is less than 1, the function returns an empty string.

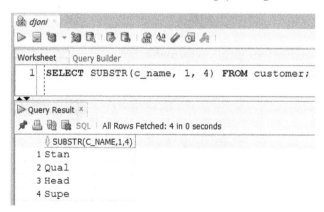

Datetime Functions

The following are some of the more important datetime functions.

CURRENT_DATE

CURRENT_DATE() returns the current date (the current date of the Oracle server at the time you run the query). For instance, the following query

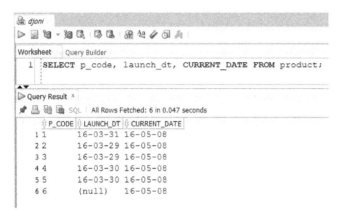

TO_CHAR

TO_CHAR(*dt*, *fmt_specifier*) converts a date (*dt*) to a string in the format specified by *fmt_specifier*. In the following example, the launch_dt column is formatted with a format specifier that has three components:

- DD - the day of the month
- MONTH - the long name of the month in uppercase
- YYYY - the year

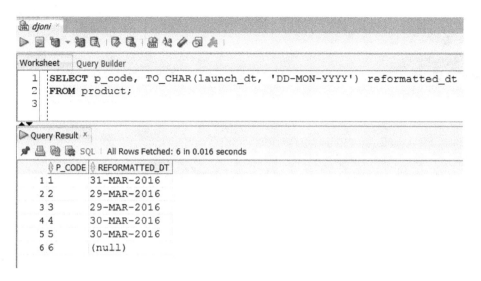

NULL-related functions

The following are some of the functions that can be used to handle null values.

COALESCE

COALESCE(*expr-1*, *expr-2*, ..., *expr-n*) returns the first expression from the list that is not NULL. For example, suppose your product table contains the following rows

For example, you want to view a computed sale_price column of the products using this formula:

- If price is available (not NULL) then discount it by 10%
- If price is not available then return 0

You can use COALESCE to produce the correct sale_price values.

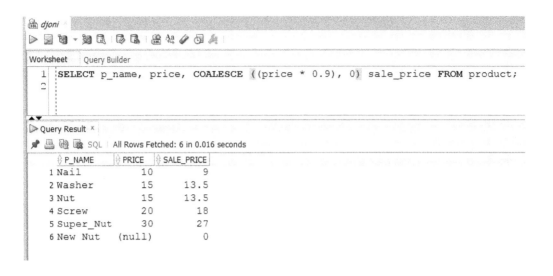

NULLIF

NULLIF (*expr1*, *expr2*) compares *expr1* and *expr2*. If they are equal, the function returns null. If they are not equal, the function returns *expr1*.

In the following query, if the price * 2 equals 30 then show the price as NULL.

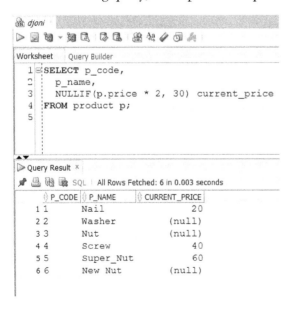

NVL

NVL (*expr1*, *expr2*) returns *exprs1* if *expr1* is not NULL; otherwise, it returns *expr2*.

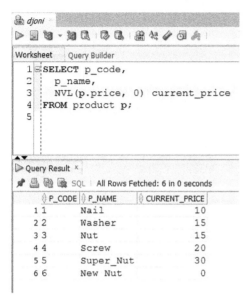

Part II: PL/SQL

While Part I is all about SQL, in this part, Part II, which has four chapters, you will learn the fundamentals of PL/SQL.

Chapter 8: Block

PL/SQL is a block-structured programming language. A PL/SQL program consists of one or more blocks. (You will later learn about multiple-blocks in the **Nesting Block** section of this chapter)

A block has three parts: Declaration, Executable and Exception-handling. A block has the following structure.

```
DECLARE
   Declaration
BEGIN
   Executable
EXCEPTION
   Exception-handling
END;
```

The three parts of a block are separated by the DECLARE, BEGIN, EXCEPTION, and END PL/SQL reserved words. You should not use any reserved word for any other than its designated purpose.

Declaration Part

Variables used to hold **program** data are declared in the Declaration part. (Data stored in a database must be read into program variables to be processed in the program)

All declaration statements must be located between the DECLARATION and BEGIN reserved words.

The syntax of a variable declaration is.

```
variable data_type;
```

Example 8-1 declares three numeric variables (a, b, and d) and one string variable c. When you run the program, it will complete successfully as indicated by the message on the Script Output pane.

The dbms_output.put_line displays the string held by c concatened with d as shown on the Dbms Output pane at the bottom of the screenshot.

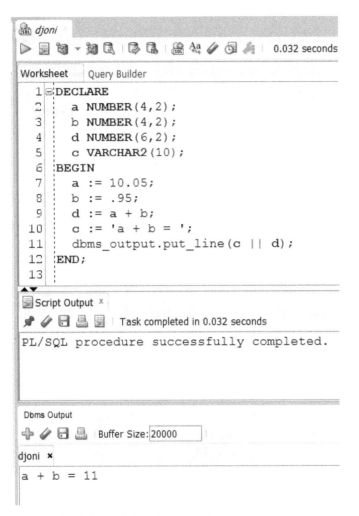

Example 8-1 Variable declarations

The Declaration part is optional, but any variable used in Executable part must be declared; otherwise, the program will fail as demonstrated in Example 8-2.

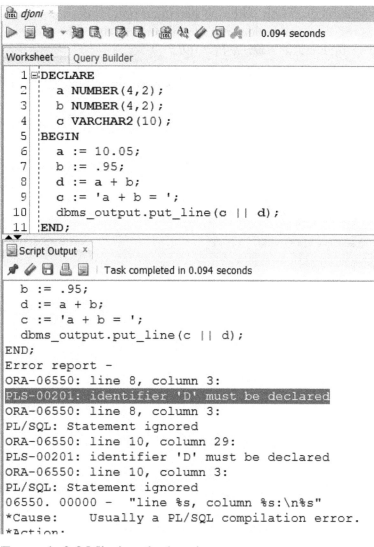

Example 8-2 Missing declaration

Executable Part

A block must have an Executable part, which in turn must have at least one statement. The Declaration and Exception-handling parts are optional.

Example 8-3 has the Executable part only with one statement only. It does not require any declaration as the Executable does not require any variable. The program successfully displays the string literal *Welcome to PL/SQL!*

Example 8-3 Mandatory executable part

Exception-handling Part

The Exception-handling part allows you to specify the actions to execute when the program encounters a runtime error.

Line 4 of Example 8-4 tries to assign a literal that is six characters long to the x variable that is declared with maximum length of five characters. When you run the program, it will abort.

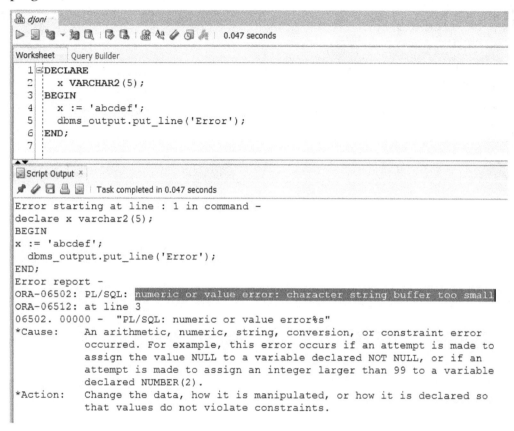

Example 8-4 Run time failure

You can avoid the failure by adding an exception handler.

In Example 8-5 below, thanks to the VALUE_ERROR exception handler, the program will get completed successfully, it does not abort. The Dbms Output has the error message you would like to be shown when a runtime exception occurs.

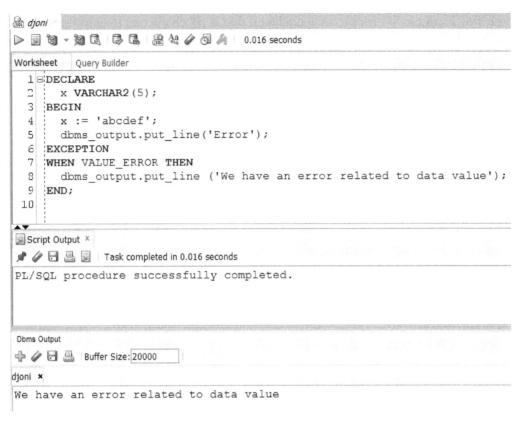

Example 8-5 Exception handler

Block Nesting

You can write a program with multiple blocks by nesting a block under another block.

In the following Example 8-6 the executable part has a total of four blocks with three levels of nesting. Line 1 – 12 is the outermost (parent) block; it is the first level of nesting. The parent block has two (children) nested blocks; they are the second level of nesting. Line 3 – 5 is the first child and line 6 – 11 is the second child. Line 8 – 10 is a (grandchild) nested block within the second child; the grandchild is at the third level of nesting.

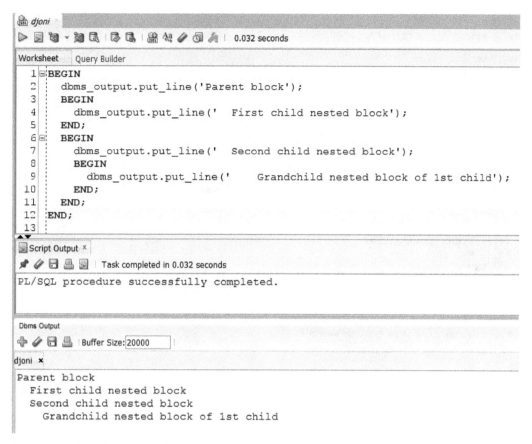

Example 8-6 Bock nesting

Block Label

You label a block at its beginning with <<*label*>> syntax and at the end with END *label*. The label at the end is optional, but having it there clarifies the block's scope: all parts and their statements of the block are those between its beginning label and end label pair.

All four blocks in the following program are labeled. In this example, each of the blocks has only one executable statement; they could well have as many statements and as complex as the program needs to.

A label is not an executable statement; Example 8-7 below produces the same result as Example 8-6.

Example 8.7 Block labels

Variable Visibility

A variable is visible (can be used) in all its nested blocks. In Example 8-8, the parent_var declared on line 3 is visible in its child's block (line 11).

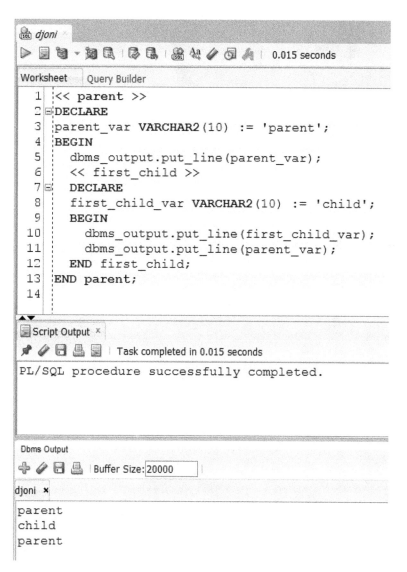

Example 8-8 Variable visibility

However, a variable declared in a nested block is neither visible to its parent block nor to other children blocks, as demonstrated in Example 8-9 below where first_child_var is not accessible by the statement on line 6 and the statement of line 16.

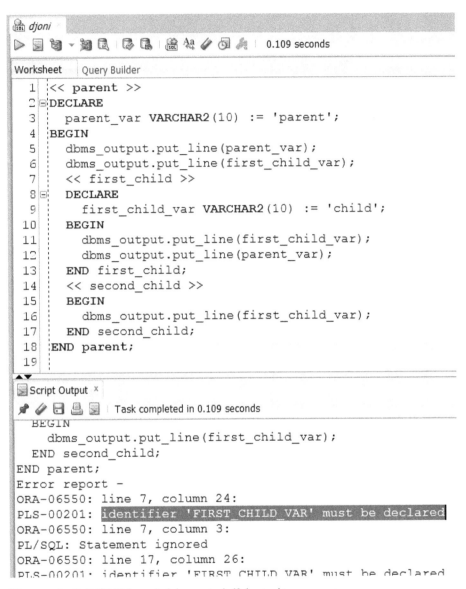

Example 8-9 Child variable not visible to its parents

Same-Name Variables

If you have a variable with the same name in two blocks, you can refer to which one of the variable by using their labels with a dot notation. The parent.same_name_var in Example 8-10 is an example. The statement on line 11 displays the value of the parent's same_name_var.

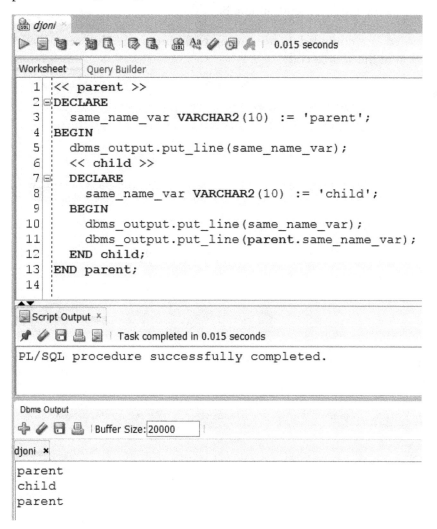

```
 1  << parent >>
 2  DECLARE
 3     same_name_var VARCHAR2(10) := 'parent';
 4  BEGIN
 5     dbms_output.put_line(same_name_var);
 6     << child >>
 7     DECLARE
 8        same_name_var VARCHAR2(10) := 'child';
 9     BEGIN
10        dbms_output.put_line(same_name_var);
11        dbms_output.put_line(parent.same_name_var);
12     END child;
13  END parent;
14
```

Script Output ×

Task completed in 0.015 seconds

```
PL/SQL procedure successfully completed.
```

Dbms Output

Buffer Size: 20000

djoni ×

```
parent
child
parent
```

Example 8-10 Same name variables

Comment

Any text in a source code following a double dash -- is a single-line comment. When a /* mark is encountered, all lines that follow until a closing */ mark is a multi-line comment.

Example 8-11 has two single-line comments on the top, two single-comments on line 4 and 5, which do not start at the beginning of the lines, and one multiline comment, which starts on line 7 and end on line 8.

Comments are ignored, not compiled, hence not part of a program. They serve as inline documentation in the source code.

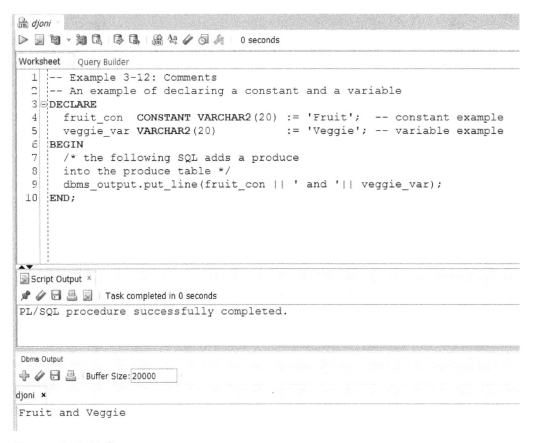

Example 8-11 Comments

Chapter 9: Variable Declaration

Variable is already introduced earlier. A variable is used to hold (store) **program** data. Here is the syntax again:

```
variable datatype;
```

A variable name must start with a letter; the rest can be letters, digits, or any of the following three symbols: _ (underscore), # (number sign), and $ (dollar sign). The maximum length of a name is 30 characters. Additionally, PL/SQL is not case sensitive.

The following four variable names, for example, are not valid.

```
9code_var -- start with numeric
Name_var% -- has a % character
price var -- has a blank
Date_the_price_of_this_produce_was_changed_var -- longer than 30
characters
```

Data Type

When you declare a variable, you must specify its datatype.

We have used the following five datatypes in Chapter 3:
- INTEGER to store numeric integer type of data
- CHAR to store fixed length string of characters
- VARCHAR2(m) to store a variable length string of characters to a maximum of m characters
- NUMBER(p, s) to store numeric data with precision of p digits and scale of s digits
- DATE to store date

Other Data Types

In addition to these five data types, PL/SQL supports other data types such as FLOAT (floating point number) and CLOB (Character Large Object Binary). Please consult the Oracle manuals available online on the Oracle website about the other data types not covered in this book.

Assignment Operator

The use of the assignment operator := to store data into a variable is demonstrated on line 4 of the following Example 9-1 program, where a literal 'Grape' is assigned to fruit_var variable.

Example 9-1 Assignment operator

Initial Value

An initial value can be assigned to a variable; its syntax is:

```
variable data_type := 'initial_value';
```

If an initialized variable is then used without changing its initial value, the initial value is applied as-is; in other words, the initial value is the default value of the variable.

Hence, an alternative syntax for the same purpose, with the DEFAULT reserved word instead of the := operator, is:

```
variable data_type DEFAULT 'initial_value';
```

In Example 9-2 below line 3 declaration initializes the fruit_var variable to an initial value, 'Grape'.

Example 9-2 Initializing variable

If a variable is not initialized, it is NULL (NULL means absence of value)

NOT NULL

You can assure a variable to always hold a value by adding a clause NOT NULL; such a variable must be initialized. Its syntax is hence as follows.

```
variable data_type NOT NULL := 'initial_value';
```

In Example 9-3 below, a is declared as NOT NULL, and it is initialized to 1. Line 7 statement fails to assign NULL to a.

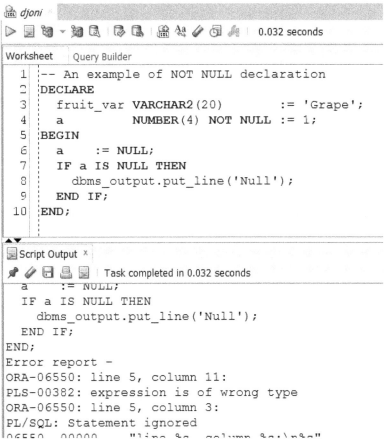

Example 9-3 Specifying NOT NULL

Constant

A constant is a 'variable' that holds a value for life, you cannot change the value; its declaration syntax is:

```
constant_name CONSTANT data_type := 'constant_value';
```

You can then use the constant_name in the Executable part to represent the constant_value. Example 9-4 has a constant declaration.

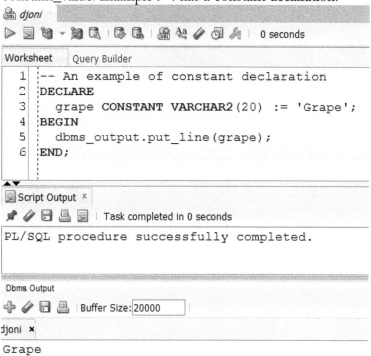

Example 9-4 CONSTANT declaration

You should not change the value of a variable declared as constant. Line 6 in the following Example 9-5 program fails trying to change the value of the grape constant.

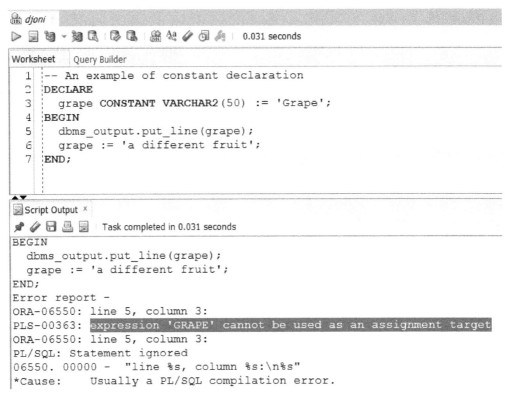

Example 9-5 Constant cannot change value

Chapter 10: Executable Statement

Here is the block structure again.

```
DECLARE
   Declaration
BEGIN
   Executable
EXCEPTION
   Exception handler
END;
```

All executable statements must be located between the BEGIN and EXCEPTION reserved words. As the Exception-handler part is optional, if a program does not have it, then all executable statements must be located between the BEGIN and END reserved words.

Assignment, Computation, and Calling Procedure

Assignment, computation, and calling procedure are executable statements. You have seen their use in earlier chapters. Example 10-1 is applying them.

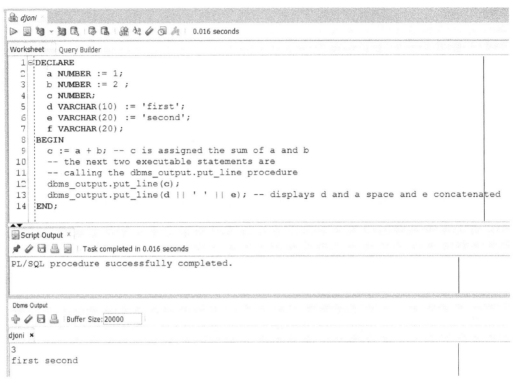

Example 10-1 Assignment, computation, calling procedure

Control Statements

To control program flows, you use conditional and loop statements: IF THEN ELSE, LOOP and CASE.

IF THEN ELSE

The syntax of the IF THEN ELSE statement is as follows. The ELSE is optional.

```
IF condition THEN
  if_statements;
ELSE else_statements;
END IF;
```

An IF THEN ELSE executes its if_statements if the condition is true. If the condition is false, the else_statements are executed.

When you run the following program (Example 10-2), you will be prompted to enter a number that will be stored in the num variable. (To prompt an input value use & as a prefix to the prompt label. If you want to prompt for a string/alphanumeric value, surround the prompt label with single quotes, for example, '&var_input').

Only if you enter a numeric value > 10, line 5 will be executed.

Example 10-2 IF THEN ELSE

IF THEN ELSIF

If you need multiple ELSE's, then use an IF THEN ELSIF statement. Its syntax is as follows.

```
IF condition_1 THEN
  statements_1;
ELSIF condition_2 THEN
  statements_2;
ELSIF ...
[ ELSE
  else_statements ]
END IF;
```

The IF THEN ELSIF statement executes only the first statement for which its condition is true; the remaining conditions are not evaluated. If no condition is true, then the else_statements are executed, if they exist; otherwise, the IF THEN ELSIF statement does nothing. The ELSE is optional.

Example 10-3 has an IF THEN ELSIF statement on lines 5 – 11. Its output depends on the input you enter on the prompt. If you enter a value greater than 10 then line 6 is executed; if equal to 10 than line 8 is executed; if less than 10, line 10 will be executed.

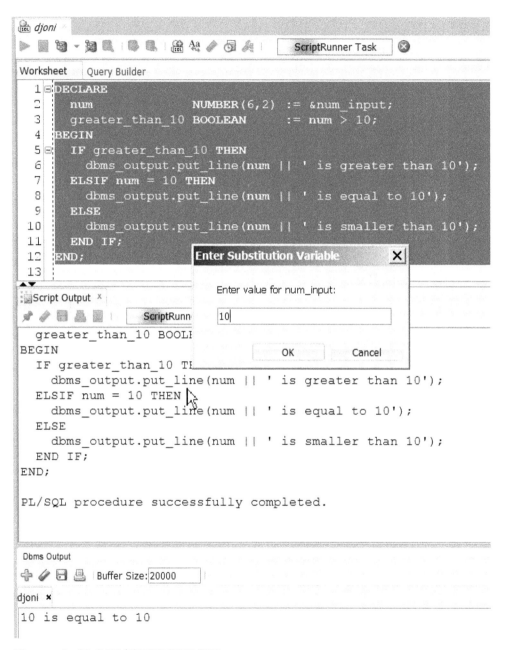

Example 10-3 IF THEN ELSIF

LOOP

Use LOOP to repeat the execution of statements within the loop.

The structure of the LOOP is

```
<<label>> LOOP
first_statement;
statement2;
...
last_statement;
END LOOP;
```

The statements run from the first to the last before the END LOOP, and then back to the first, until an EXIT conditional statement, which should be provided within the loop, is satisfied on which the loop is terminated.

The label is optional, but it helps clarifies the scope of the loop.

The loop in Example 10-4 iterates line 9 – 10 three times. On the fourth iteration num = 4, the exit condition on line 6 is satisfied, hence the next statement after the loop on line 13 is executed, and then the program ends.

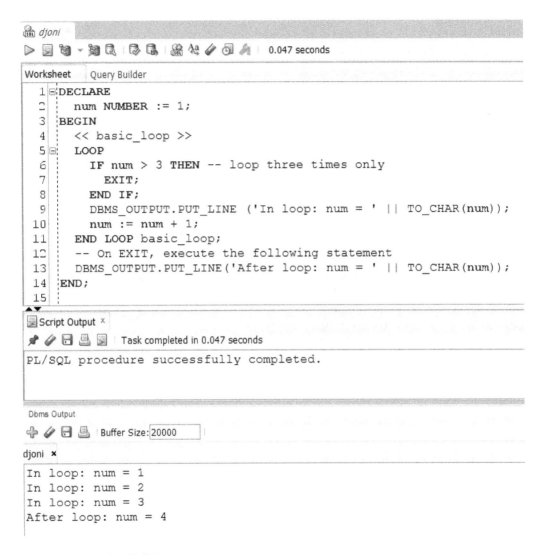

Example 10-4 LOOP

Nested LOOP

You can nest a loop. In Example 10-5 the inner loop on line 10 - 15 is nested within the outer loop that starts on line 5. For every cycle of the outer loop, the inner loop is iterated twice.

Example 10-5 Nested LOOP

Fixed Number of Iteration

If you know exactly the number of iteration, you can use the following loop structure.

```
FOR i IN 1..u
  LOOP
    statements;
  END LOOP;
```

i the loop index, l the lower bound and u is the upper bound of the index. The index value starts with l when the loop is entered, and increments by 1; the last iteration is when the index reaches u.

Look at Example 10-6. The dbms_output.put_line statement inside the loop is executed three times as for this example i= 1 and u = 3.

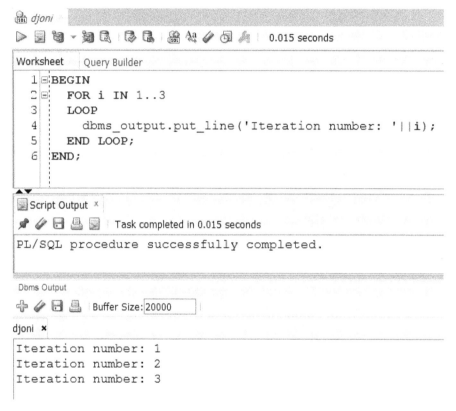

Example 10-6 Fixed number interation

WHILE Loop

You can also use a WHILE to form a loop. Its syntax is as follows.

```
WHILE condition
LOOP
statements;
END LOOP;
```

The statements in the loop will be executed as long as the condition is true. You must ensure the loop can terminate.

Example 10-7 does the same as Example 10-6; its loop terminates when i = 4. Notice that the i variable used here must be declared; while with LOOP as in Example 10-6 should not be. The i variable is incremented on line 6, which will terminate the loop when its value reaches 4.

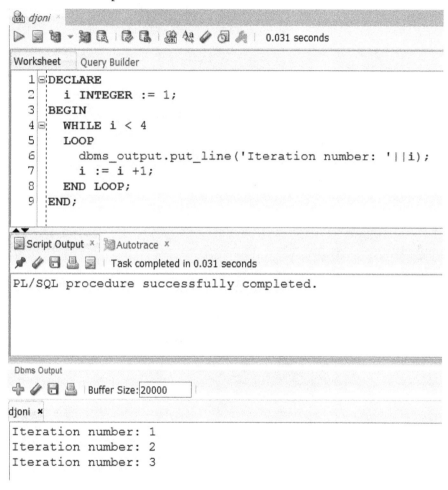

Example 10-7 WHILE loop

CASE

CASE is similar to IF THEN ELSIF. CASE comes in two flavors: Simple and Searched.

Simple CASE

The syntax of the Simple CASE statement is.

```
CASE selector
WHEN selector_value_1 THEN statements_1
WHEN selector_value_2 THEN statements_2
WHEN ...
[ ELSE else_statements ]
END CASE;
```

The selector is a variable. Each selector_value can be either a literal or a variable.

The simple CASE statement runs the first statement for which its selector_value equals the selector. Remaining conditions are not evaluated. If no selector_value equals selector, the CASE statement runs else_statements if they exist; or raises the predefined exception CASE_NOT_FOUND otherwise.

The ELSE is optional.

Look at Example 10-8.

The selector in the following Simple CASE statement is the variable *clue*. The statement has three WHEN's, each with a literal as its selector value; the first WHEN's selector value, for example, is literal 'O'.

If the clue value you enter on the prompt is not any one of the selector value's, the ELSE statement, line 14, will be executed.

Example 10-8 Simple CASE

Searched CASE

A Searched CASE statement has the following syntax.

CASE

```
WHEN condition_1 THEN statements_1
WHEN condition_2 THEN statements_2
WHEN...
ELSE else_statements
END CASE;
```

While in the Simple CASE, the "condition" of selecting which statements to execute is comparing the selection_value to the selector for equality, in Searched CASE the condition is within each WHEN.

The conditions are independent; they do not need to have any kind of relationship.

Two or more conditions can be true, but only the first in the order you have in the source program (top to bottom) will be granted and its statements executed.

The following Example 10-9 demonstrates a Searched CASE. When you run the program, you will be prompted twice to enter the value for clue1 and then for clue2. One of the WHEN's or the ELSE is executed depending your inputs.

```
 1  DECLARE
 2     clue1 VARCHAR2(1) := '&clue1_input';
 3     clue2 VARCHAR2(1) := '&clue2_input';
 4     BEGIN
 5     CASE
 6     WHEN clue1 = 'O' THEN
 7        DBMS_OUTPUT.PUT_LINE('Obvious');
 8     WHEN (clue1 = 'U' OR clue2 = 'U') THEN
 9        DBMS_OUTPUT.PUT_LINE('Useless');
10     WHEN (clue1 = 'N' AND clue2 = 'N') THEN
11        DBMS_OUTPUT.PUT_LINE('Not Sure');
12     ELSE
13        DBMS_OUTPUT.PUT_LINE('Input Not Valid');
14     END CASE;
15  END;
```

Example 10-9 Searched CASE

Chapter 11: Exception-handling

You have been introduced to Exception handling in Chapter 8.

Here is the syntax of an exception handler.

```
WHEN exception THEN statements;
```

For your convenient reminder, here is the example from that chapter. Notice that the program run to its completion. Without the exception handler, it would abort at run time.

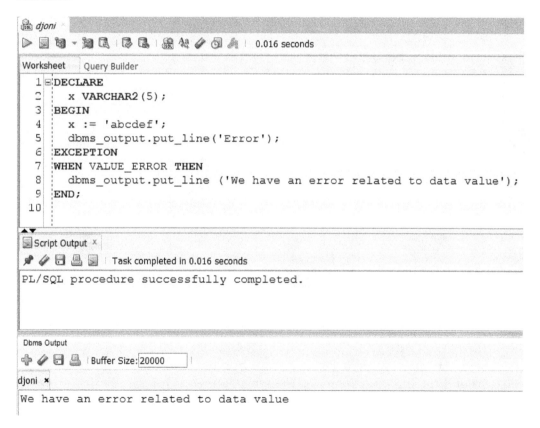

Multiple Exception-handlers

An Exception-handling part can have more than one handler. In Example 11-1 below we have added an OTHERS handler to handle any other error type.

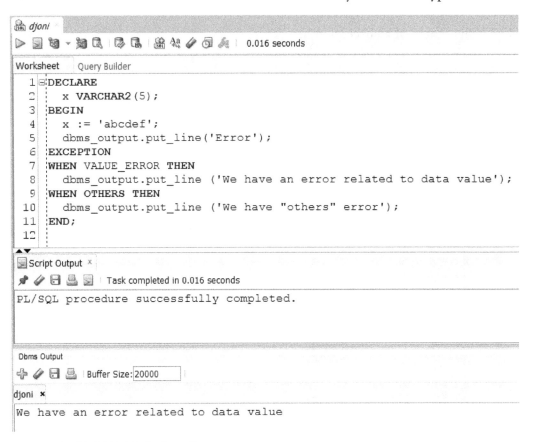

```
djoni

                                      0.016 seconds
Worksheet    Query Builder
  1 DECLARE
  2     x VARCHAR2(5);
  3 BEGIN
  4     x := 'abcdef';
  5     dbms_output.put_line('Error');
  6 EXCEPTION
  7 WHEN VALUE_ERROR THEN
  8     dbms_output.put_line ('We have an error related to data value');
  9 WHEN OTHERS THEN
 10     dbms_output.put_line ('We have "others" error');
 11 END;
 12

Script Output ×

             Task completed in 0.016 seconds
PL/SQL procedure successfully completed.

Dbms Output

              Buffer Size: 20000
djoni ×
We have an error related to data value
```

Example 11-1 Multiple handlers

Combining Exceptions

If you want the same exception action for two or more different exception-handlers, you can put them into one exception. The syntax is then as follows.

```
WHEN exception1 OR exception2 OR...
THEN exception_action
```

Example 11-2 has one exception with two handlers.

```
 djoni

Worksheet    Query Builder
   1  DECLARE
   2      x VARCHAR2(5);
   3  BEGIN
   4      x := 'abcdef';
   5      dbms_output.put_line('Error');
   6  EXCEPTION
   7  WHEN VALUE_ERROR OR OTHERS THEN
   8      dbms_output.put_line ('We have data value or other error');
   9  END;
  10
```

Example 11-2 Combining handlers

Visibility of Exception

Similar to the scope of a variable, an exception handler in a nested block is visible only within itself. On the other hand parents' exception handlers can handle its children's exceptions if they don't have the applicable handlers.

In Example 11-3, though the child has an exception handler, the parent block does not; hence its failure is not handled and the program got aborted.

Example 11-3 Child Exception non visibility

In Example 11-4, the child does not have any exception handler, but its parent has; so the child failure is handled by the parent's.

```
  1  << parent >>
  2  DECLARE
  3     x VARCHAR2(5);
  4     n NUMBER;
  5  BEGIN
  6     dbms_output.put_line('Parent');
  7     << child >>
  8     BEGIN
  9       dbms_output.put_line('Child');
 10       x := 'abcdef';
 11       n := 1/0;
 12     END child;
 13  EXCEPTION
 14  WHEN VALUE_ERROR OR ZERO_DIVIDE THEN
 15     dbms_output.put_line ('We have data-value or zero-divide error');
 16  END parent;
 17
```

Script Output ×

Task completed in 0.015 seconds

```
PL/SQL procedure successfully completed.
```

Dbms Output

Buffer Size: 20000

djoni ×

```
Parent
Child
We have data-value or zero-divide error
```

Example 11-4 Parent exception visibility

Predefined Exceptions

VALUE_EROR, ZERO_DIVIDE, and OTHERS, which you have learned so far, are examples of PL/SQL predefined exceptions.

Please consult the Oracle PL/SQL manual for a complete list of the predefined exceptions.

SQLCODE and SQLERRM functions

PL/SQL provides SQLCODE and SQLERRM functions; when you call these functions, they will return the Oracle error code and message respectively for the error encountered by your program at run time.

Example 11-5 demonstrates the use of the two functions on line 7 and 8.

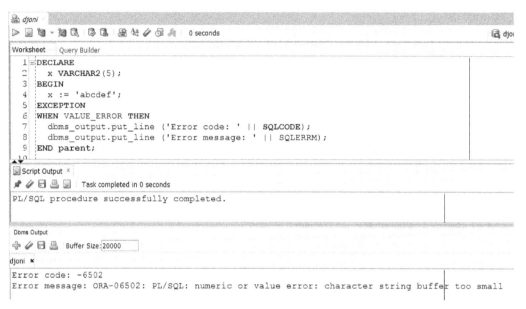

Example 11-5 SQLCODE and SQLERRM

Defining Oracle Error

You might have an error that does not have a pre-defined exception. Fortunately, PL/SQL has a feature to solve it known as PRAGMA EXCEPTION_INIT. You first declare an EXCEPTION in the Declaration part; its syntax is as follows.

```
exception EXCEPTION;
```

Then, also in the Declaration part, you define that exception with the following syntax.

```
PRAGMA EXCEPTION_INIT(exception, -Oracle_error_number);
```

where `exception_name` is the name of the exception you already declare, and the number is a negative value corresponding to an `ORA-` error number. You will need to find out this error number in the Oracle manual, or find it using the SQLCODE function as in Example 11-5.

In Example 11-6, line 6 fails to assign 39 digits value to a numeric data type which can handle up to 38 digits. The error number of the failure is -6502 that we use to define the exception named my_predef_exc.

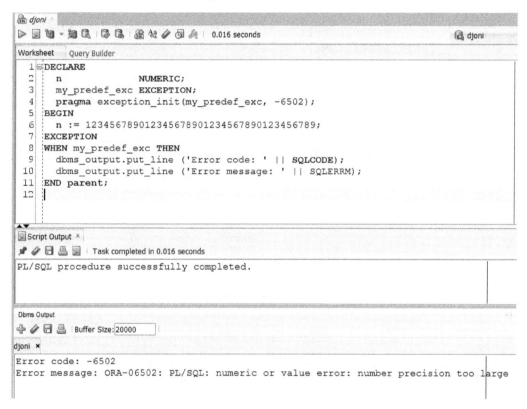

Example 11-6 Defining Oracle err

User Defined Exception

All previous exceptions were run-time errors. You can also define your own exceptions that are not run-time errors, and let the Exception part handle these user-defined exceptions in the same fashion as run-time error exceptions.

You declare your own exception, use it using RAISE clause, and in the Exception part specify what to do.

In Example 11-7, we declare an exception we name too_large on line 3, raise it on line 6, and show a message on line 10.

Example 11-7 User defined exception

Part III SQL and PL/SQL together

In Part I you learned SQL and Part II, PL/SQL program. In this part, Part III, you will learn that PL/SQL programs can have SQL statements.

You will notice that we will, in this part, use different tables than those we used in Part I.

Chapter 12: Using SQL in PL/SQL

Let's start by putting in DDL statements. The purpose of Example 12-1 is to increase price by 10% of the average price on the products that have prices lower than average unit price.

Example 12-1 has two SQL statements, a SELECT statement and an UPDATE statement.

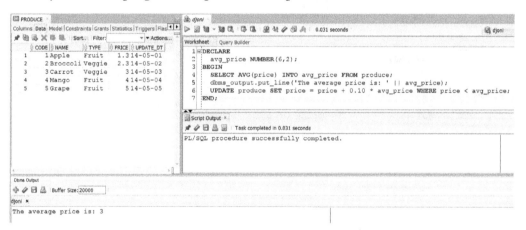

Example 12-1 DDL statements in PL/SQL program

When you run the program, the prices on the produce table will be as follows.

PL/SQL Advantage over SQL's

When you run a PL/SQL program, such as Example 12-1, all lines of statements are sent to the database at once. All SQL statements will be sent together. All results will also be sent back once, such as all output displays by the dbms_output.put_line back to the SQL Developer. Such PL/SQL program with more than one SQL statement will likely be executed faster than submitting one statement after another.

INTO clause

Note that the SELECT statement must have an INTO clause, which is applicable only within PL/SQL programs.

The SELECT with INTO syntax is

```
SELECT select_columns INTO into_columns FROM ...
```

The into_columns must be in the sequence and the same datatype as those of the select_columns. The preceding Example 12-2 has a SELECT statement that has three INTO columns.

Only One Row

A SELECT INTO must return exactly one row. Example 12-4 fails as its query returns more than one row.

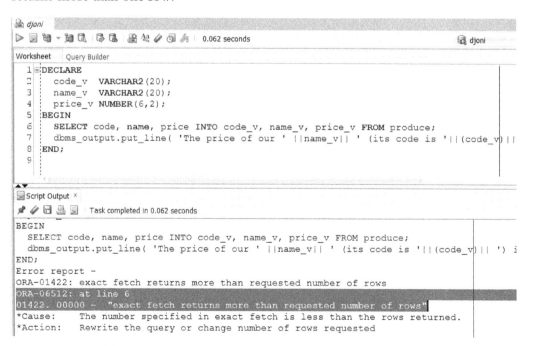

Example 12-2 Too many rows exception

ROWTYPE and TYPE

PL/SQL provides two special datatypes to make sure the variables you use as the INTO columns are correctly the same as the table's columns. The syntax of the ROWTYPE and TYPE datatypes syntaxes are respectively:

```
variable_name table_name%ROWTYPE;

variable_name column_name%TYPE;
```

You use ROWTYPE to at once refer to all the columns of the table; while the TYPE refers to a specific column.

Example 12-3 uses these two datatypes. The avg_price has the unit_price column's datatype of the produce table. The p_row consists of columns that match the produce table's columns; for example, the first column, p_row.code has the same datatype as that of produce.code. Note the use of dot notation to refer to a column.

Example 12-3 ROWTYPE and TYPE

SELECT for UPDATE

When you need to first SELECT and then UPDATE the selected row, and you want to be sure the selected row is not updated by any other SQL statement while you are updating it, you can lock the selected row using a SELECT for UPDATE statement as demonstrated in Example 12-4.

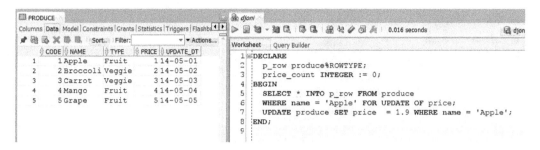

When you run the program, the Apple's price will be updated to 1.9.

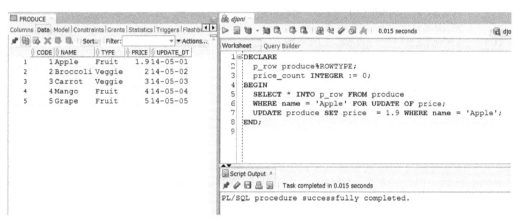

Example 12-4 SELECT FOR UPDATE

Commit and Rollback

A COMMIT statement commits new, deleted and updates rows persistently in the database. You can issue a ROLLBACK statement to back out changes that have not been committed.

Example 12-5 has both the COMMIT and ROLLBACK statements. The update to the Apple's price is committed if it is the only produce with 1.9 price (which is true); otherwise, the update is roll-backed.

```
djoni
Worksheet      Query Builder
   1  DECLARE
   2    p_row produce%ROWTYPE;
   3    price_count INTEGER := 0;
   4  BEGIN
   5    SELECT * INTO p_row FROM produce
   6    WHERE name = 'Apple' FOR UPDATE OF price;
   7    UPDATE produce SET price  = 1.9 WHERE name = 'Apple';
   8    SELECT COUNT(*) INTO price_count FROM produce
   9    WHERE price    = 1.9;
  10    IF price_count > 1 THEN
  11       ROLLBACK;
  12    ELSE
  13       COMMIT;
  14    END IF;
  15  END;
  16
```

Example 12-5 Commit and Rollback

Note that your program can also have a DELETE statement.

Transaction

A transaction is a group of SQL statements. You control the grouped statements so that the data changes they have effected are committed (applied to the database persistently) using a COMMIT statement, or rolled back (undone from the database) using a ROLLBACK statement.

The program in Example 12-6 has two UPDATE statements that change the data of the produce table. The first update starts a transaction. If, after the price updates, the average price is higher than 10.00, the two updates would be rolled back; otherwise they are committed. The commit ends the transaction.

```
djoni
 ▷ 🖫 🖺 ▾ 🛢 🖪  🖪 🖪  🞖 📇 ⚟ ✏ 🖫 🞝   0.093 seconds                    🖫 djoni
Worksheet   Query Builder
  1 ⊟DECLARE
  2 ┊  avgprc NUMBER(6,2);
  3 ┊BEGIN
  4 ┊  SELECT AVG(price) INTO avgprc FROM PRODUCE;
  5 ┊  UPDATE produce SET price = price + (price * 0.10) WHERE price < avgprc;
  6 ┊  UPDATE produce SET price = price + (price * 0.01) WHERE price > avgprc;
  7 ┊  SELECT AVG(price) INTO avgprc FROM produce;
  8 ┊  IF avgprc > 10.00 THEN
  9 ┊    ROLLBACK;
 10 ┊  END IF;
 11 ┊  COMMIT;
 12 ┊END;
```

Example 12-6 Transaction

Savepoint

Within a transaction you can set a savepoint to set the boundary of a rollback. In Example 12-7 we set a savepoint named after_insert after the INSERT statement. When a rollback occurs the changes rolled back to only right before the SAVEPOINT statement, i.e. only the insert is roll backed, first update is not

```
djoni
 ▷ 🖫 🖺 ▾ 🛢 🖪  🖪 🖪  🞖 📇 ⚟ ✏ 🖫 🞝   0.125 seconds                    🖫 djoni
Worksheet   Query Builder
  1 ⊟DECLARE
  2 ┊  avgprc NUMBER(6,2);
  3 ┊BEGIN
  4 ┊  SELECT AVG(price) INTO avgprc FROM PRODUCE;
  5 ┊  UPDATE produce SET price = price + (price * 0.10) WHERE price < avgprc;
  6 ⊟  INSERT
  7 ┊  INTO produce VALUES
  8 ┊    (
  9 ┊      999,'Kale',
 10 ┊      'V',1.50,
 11 ┊      to_date('1-5-2013','DD-MM-YYYY')
 12 ┊    );
 13 ┊  SAVEPOINT after_insert;
 14 ┊  UPDATE produce SET price = price + (price * 0.10) WHERE price > avgprc;
 15 ┊  SELECT AVG(price) INTO avgprc FROM produce;
 16 ┊  IF avgprc > 2.00 THEN
 17 ┊    ROLLBACK TO after_insert;
 18 ┊  END IF;
 19 ┊  COMMIT;
 20 ┊END;
```

Example 12-7 Savepoint

Multiple Transactions

A program can have more than one transaction. You start a transaction by issuing a SET TRANSACTION statement and end it by a COMMIT or ROLLBACK statement.

The SET TRANSACTION has the following syntax.

```
SET TRANSACTION 'transaction';
```

The program in Example 12-8 has two transactions: t1 and t2. When the rollback happens, the changes rolled back is only within t2.

```
1  DECLARE
2    avgprc NUMBER(6,2);
3  BEGIN
4    SET TRANSACTION NAME 't1';
5    INSERT
6    INTO produce VALUES
7      (
8        9,'Mellon',
9        'F',5.50,
10       to_date('1-5-2013','DD-MM-YYYY')
11     );
12   COMMIT;
13   SET transaction name 't2';
14   UPDATE produce SET price = price + (price * 0.10) WHERE price > avgprc;
15   SELECT AVG(price) INTO avgprc FROM produce;
16   IF avgprc > 12.00 THEN
17     ROLLBACK;
18   END IF;
19   COMMIT;
20 END;
21
```

Example 12-8 Setting transaction

DDL (Data Definition Language)

All the above SQL statements are DML statements (Data Manipulation Language). You can also have DDL statements (Data Definition Language) in PL/SQL program.

Inside a PL/SQL program, you use the EXECUTE IMMEDIATE statement to pass a DDL statement. The EXECUTE IMMEDIATE statement has the following syntax.

EXECUTE IMMEDIATE ('DDL statement');

Example 12-9 has a CREATE TABLE statement (line 2). When you run the program, the sample_produce table will be created.

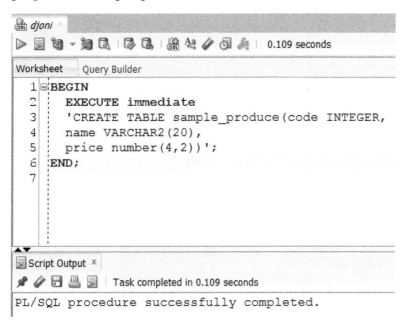

Example 12-9 DDL statement

Note that the DDL statement is quoted; in the PL/SQL program it is a string literal (value).

Chapter 13: Cursor

A cursor is the storage of **rows** returned by the cursor's query. You define the cursor's **query** when you declare the cursor. The syntax of a declaring a cursor is:

DECLARE CURSOR *cursor_name* IS **query**;

Once a cursor is declared you can use it follows. In the executable part, open the cursor; fetch its rows sequentially, when you are done with the cursor, close it. The syntax of the OPEN, FETCH, and CLOSE statements are respectively:

OPEN cursor_name;

FETCH cursor_name INTO variables;

CLOSE cursor_name;

The INTO **variables** clause in the FETCH statement stores the columns of a cursor's row into the **variables**. All data types of the variables must match with the data types of the columns of the rows.

In Example 13-1 a cursor named c is declared on line 2 – 4. Its query returns all rows from the produce table.

To match the data types of the cursor's columns, the v_produce variable used on line 8 to store the cursor's row is declared as the cursor's row type using the %rowtype data typing, for other rowtype kinds of data type).

Please truncate the produce table and insert the five initial rows.

When you run Example 13-1, as the FETCH is executed only once only the first row is fetched and displayed.

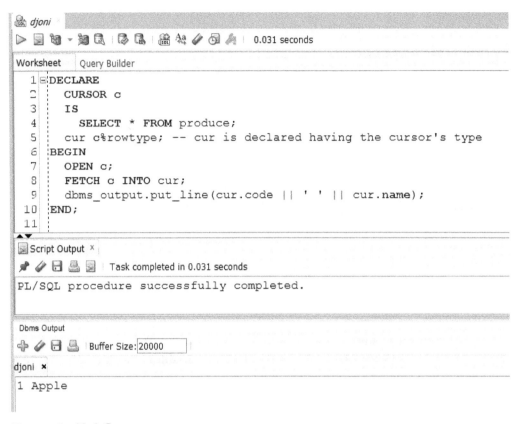

Example 13-1 Cursor

Cursor Parameters

A cursor can have parameters in its query. Our c cursor now (in Example 13-2) has a low and high parameters (line 2). We pass values to the parameters when we open the cursor (line 8).

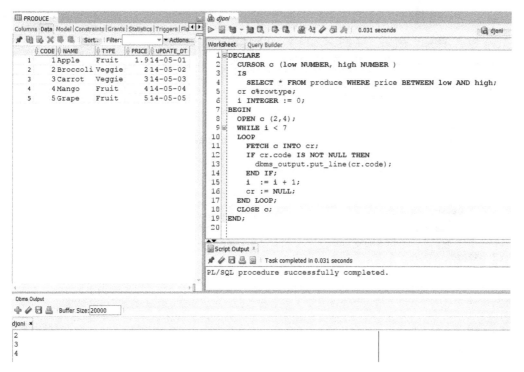

Example 13-2 Parameters

PL/SQL Variable in the Query

A cursor's query can include PL/SQL variable.

The cursor's query in Example 13-3 uses price_increase variable in its second output column. This column is added to the produce's unit_price; the sum is aliased as new_price.

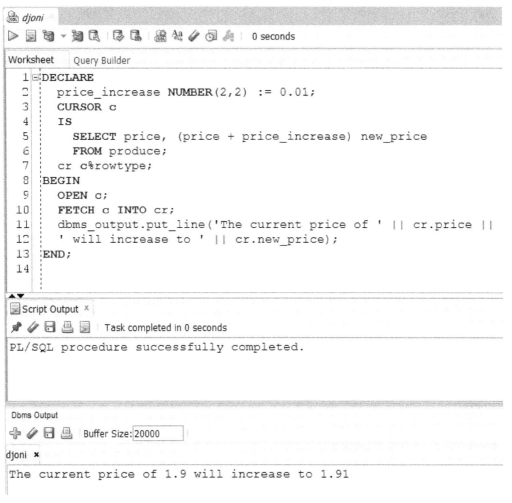

Example 13-3 PL/SQL variable

Cursor Last Row

Fetching beyond the last row does not produce any error, the value in the INTO variable is still that from last rows fetched.

Example 13-4 will be completed successfully. The loop iterates six times. As the produce table has five rows only and code 5 is the last code fetched, the 5th and the 6th outputs are 5.

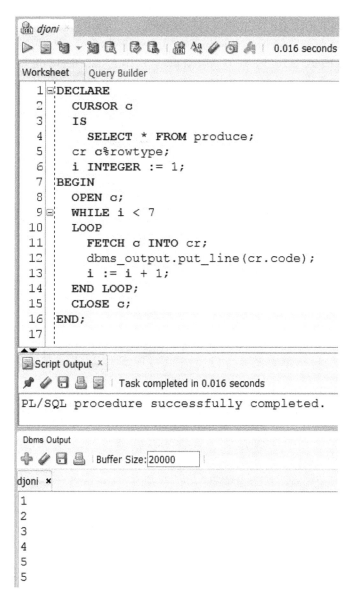

Example 13-4 Last row fetched

Cursor Attributes

PL/SQL provides %ISOPEN, %FOUND, %NOTFOUND, and %ROWCOUNT attributes.

As you will not generally know in advance the number of rows in a cursor, you don't know when to stop the loop iteration. Fortunately you can use the %NOTFOUND cursor attribute to detect when there is no more row in a cursor. In Example 13-5, the "EXIT WHEN %NOTFOUND" statement (line 10 - 11) stops the loop from fetching further beyond the last row.

Example 13-5 Cursor attribute

Cursor FOR Loop

The cursor FOR loop specifies a sequence of statements to be repeated once for each row returned by a cursor. Use the cursor FOR loop if you need to process every record from a cursor; it does not need you to open, fetch and close the cursor.

In Example 13-6, using the c_index (a variable that you don't need to declare), the for-loop on line 8 – 11, displays the code and name of every Veggie produce from the cursor.

```sql
DECLARE
   CURSOR c
   IS
      SELECT code, name
      FROM produce
      WHERE type = 'Veggie';
BEGIN
   FOR c_index IN c
   LOOP
      dbms_output.put_line(c_index.code ||' '|| c_index.name);
   END LOOP;
END;
```

Script Output

Task completed in 0.016 seconds

```
PL/SQL procedure successfully completed.
```

Dbms Output

Buffer Size: 20000

djoni ×

```
2 Broccoli
3 Carrot
```

Example 13-6 FOR LOOP

Cursor FOR LOOP short cut

A statement with the following syntax effectively loops through the rows returned by the query.

```
FOR returned_rows IN
  (query)
  LOOP
    statements;
  END LOOP;
```

No cursor is declared. You don't need to declare the returned_rows which stores the query's returned rows. The loop iterates through all rows returned by the query.

In Example 13-7 all rows from the produce table are returned. These rows are all processed one by one sequentially. Each of the output string, the produce's type and name, to be displayed is constructed on line 7.

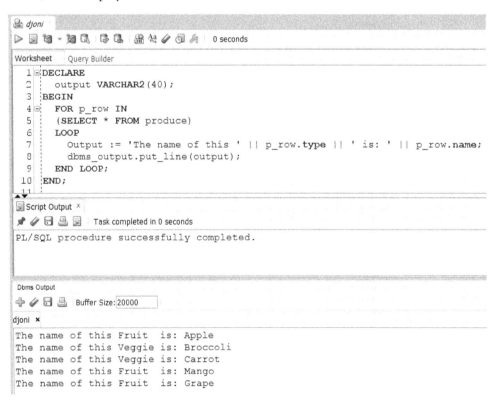

Example 13-7 FOR LOOP shortcut

Chapter 14: Subprogram

A program might need to execute the same statements in more than one place. Rather than having the same statements repeated in those places, you can define the statements once as a subprogram. You can then just call the subprogram in the places where it is needed.

Subprogram can be a function or a procedure.

Function

A function, when called, returns a value.

In the Declaration part of the program you specify the function using the following structure.

```
DECLARE
  FUNCTION function (parameters)
    RETURN data_type
  IS
    variables; -- if any is needed in the Executable part
    BEGIN
    Executable statements; -- what the function does
    RETURN value; -- you can have more than one RETURN
    EXCEPTION
    Exception_handlers;
    END function;
```

In the above structure, the function has its own block shown bold-highlighted. Notice that though the function block does not have its own DECLARE, if the function need any variable you can declare the variables after the IS reserved word. The value of the RETURN statement is returned (produced) when the function is called.

Example 14-1 is a program that has a function named *uc_name*. The function converts and returns the name of a produce in uppercase.

You identify the produce by specifying its code in the parameter of the function. The parameter *code_p* has the datatype of the produce's code column.

The SELECT statement (line 8) retrieves the produce name that has its code = code_p. The produce name converted to uppercase is stored into the name_uc variable.

When the function encounters any error during its run time, its OTHERS exception handler's returns an 'Error'.

You call the function as follows: uc_name (*code_p*).

The function is called twice, first on line 17, then on line 20. The first call is in the FOR LOOP (line 19 – 25). The dbms_output.put_line in the loop produces the list of all produce names in uppercase.

The second call tests if produce code 9 exists in the table; if it does not, 'Error' will be displayed.

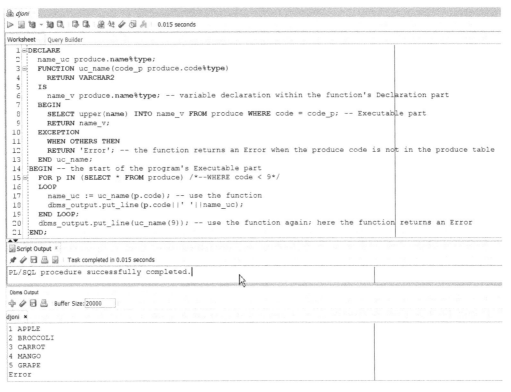

```
 1  DECLARE
 2    name_uc produce.name%type;
 3    FUNCTION uc_name(code_p produce.code%type)
 4      RETURN VARCHAR2
 5    IS
 6      name_v produce.name%type; -- variable declaration within the function's Declaration part
 7    BEGIN
 8      SELECT upper(name) INTO name_v FROM produce WHERE code = code_p; -- Executable part
 9      RETURN name_v;
10    EXCEPTION
11      WHEN OTHERS THEN
12        RETURN 'Error'; -- the function returns an Error when the produce code is not in the produce table
13    END uc_name;
14  BEGIN -- the start of the program's Executable part
15    FOR p IN (SELECT * FROM produce) /*--WHERE code < 9*/
16    LOOP
17      name_uc := uc_name(p.code); -- use the function
18      dbms_output.put_line(p.code||' '||name_uc);
19    END LOOP;
20    dbms_output.put_line(uc_name(9)); -- use the function again; here the function returns an Error
21  END;
```

Script Output ×

Task completed in 0.015 seconds

PL/SQL procedure successfully completed.

Dbms Output

Buffer Size: 20000

djoni ×

```
1 APPLE
2 BROCCOLI
3 CARROT
4 MANGO
5 GRAPE
Error
```

Example 14-1 User defined function

Procedure

While a function returns a value, a procedure does some actions. Here is the structure of a procedure.

```
DECLARE
  PROCEDURE procedure (parameters)
  IS
    variables; -- if any is needed in the Executable part
  BEGIN
    statements; -- what the function does
  END procedure;
```

The procedure update_price in Example 14-2 takes the name of a produce as a parameter and increase the produce's price by 10%. The Executable part uses the procedure twice, on line 12 and 13, to update the price of Apple and Carrot.

You call the procedure as follows: update_price (*name*).

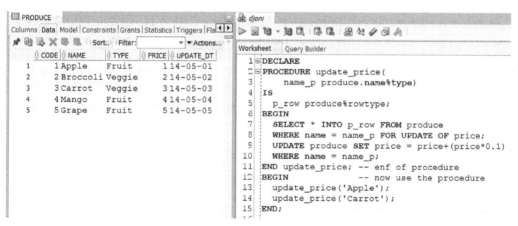

Example 14-2 User defined procedure

When you finish running Example 14-2, the prices of Apple and Carrot are as seen here.

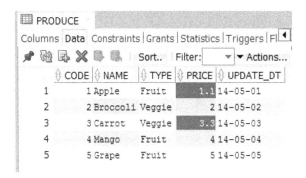

Stored Programs

The previous function and procedure are in-line; they are defined, and at the same time used, in the same programs.

You can also create them so they are stored in the database as database objects. You can then use them in any other program.

To create stored function and procedure you use the CREATE FUNCTION and CREATE PROCEDURE statements that have the following syntaxes respectively.

Example 14-3 and 14-4 show the statements to create the stored versions of our uc_name function and update_price procedure. When you run these CREATE statements the uc_name function and update_price procedure will be created and stored in the database.

```
Worksheet    Query Builder
 1 ⊟CREATE FUNCTION uc_name(
 2 ┊     cp_code produce.code%type)
 3 ┊   RETURN VARCHAR2
 4 ┊IS
 5 ┊   name_v VARCHAR2(50);
 6 ┊BEGIN
 7 ┊   SELECT upper(name) INTO name_v FROM produce WHERE code = cp_code;
 8 ┊   RETURN name_v;
 9 ┊EXCEPTION
10 ┊WHEN OTHERS THEN
11 ┊   RETURN 'Error';
12 ┊END uc_name;
13 ┊
```

Script Output ×

Task completed in 0.093 seconds

```
Function UC_NAME compiled
```

Example 14-3 Stored function

```
Worksheet    Query Builder
 1 ⊟CREATE PROCEDURE update_price(
 2 ┊     cp_name produce.name%type)
 3 ┊AS
 4 ┊   v_produce produce%rowtype;
 5 ┊BEGIN
 6 ┊   SELECT * INTO v_produce FROM produce WHERE name = cp_name FOR UPDATE OF price;
 7 ┊   UPDATE produce SET price = price+(price*0.1) WHERE name = cp_name;
 8 ┊END update_price;
 9 ┊
```

Script Output ×

Task completed in 0.093 seconds

```
Procedure UPDATE_PRICE compiled
```

Example 14-4 Stored procedure

Example 14-5 and 14-6 are programs that use the stored function and procedure respectively.

```
Worksheet    Query Builder
  1 ⊟DECLARE
  2 ┊    v_name produce.name%type;
  3 ┊BEGIN
  4 ⊟  FOR p IN
  5 ┊   (SELECT * FROM produce
  6 ┊   )
  7 ┊   LOOP
  8 ┊     v_name:=uc_name(p.code);
  9 ┊     dbms_output.put_line(p.code||' '||v_name);
 10 ┊   END LOOP;
 11 ┊END;
 1? ┊
```

Example 14-5 Using stored function

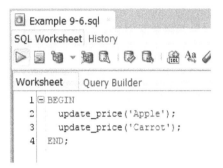

```
SQL Worksheet  History

Worksheet    Query Builder
  1 ⊟ BEGIN
  2      update_price('Apple');
  3      update_price('Carrot');
  4   END;
```

Example 14-6 Using stored procedure

Package

We can put together stored procedures and functions into a stored package. The dbms_output.put_line procedure we have been using is one of the built-in packages. Put_line is one of the procedures in the dbms_output package. We access the procedures and function in a package using a dot notation.

A package has two parts: specification and body. The specification declares the procedures and functions in the body.

Creating Package

A package has two parts: specification and body.

The mypackage packages our uc_name function and update_price package. The package specification and body are created by the statements in Example 14-7 and 14-8 respectively.

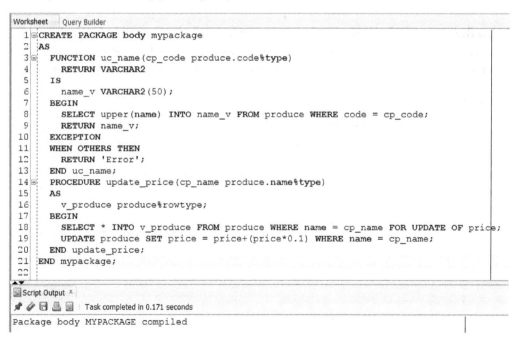

```
Worksheet    Query Builder
1  CREATE PACKAGE mypackage
2  AS
3    FUNCTION uc_name(
4        cp_code produce.code%type)
5      RETURN VARCHAR2;
6    PROCEDURE update_price(
7        cp_name produce.name%type);
8  END mypackage;
9
```

```
Script Output x
Task completed in 0.109 seconds
Package MYPACKAGE compiled
```

Example 14-7 Creating package spec

```
Worksheet    Query Builder
1  CREATE PACKAGE body mypackage
2  AS
3    FUNCTION uc_name(cp_code produce.code%type)
4      RETURN VARCHAR2
5    IS
6      name_v VARCHAR2(50);
7    BEGIN
8      SELECT upper(name) INTO name_v FROM produce WHERE code = cp_code;
9      RETURN name_v;
10   EXCEPTION
11   WHEN OTHERS THEN
12     RETURN 'Error';
13   END uc_name;
14   PROCEDURE update_price(cp_name produce.name%type)
15   AS
16     v_produce produce%rowtype;
17   BEGIN
18     SELECT * INTO v_produce FROM produce WHERE name = cp_name FOR UPDATE OF price;
19     UPDATE produce SET price = price+(price*0.1) WHERE name = cp_name;
20   END update_price;
21 END mypackage;
22
```

```
Script Output x
Task completed in 0.171 seconds
Package body MYPACKAGE compiled
```

Example 14-8 Creating package body

Trigger

A trigger is a database object that has some PL/SQL codes, which get fired (executed) in response to a specified event. The event can be, for example, a delete, insert, or update statement.

The syntax of the CREATE TRIGER is as follows.

```
CREATE TRIGGER trigger
BEFORE | AFTER
DELETE | OR INSERT | OR UPDATE
ON table
PL/SQL block
```

The t_prodlog trigger create by Example 14-9 is fired when a delete or insert statement is executed on the produce table.

You must have created the prodlog table before running the CREATE TRIGGER statement. Use the following statement to create the prodlog table.

```
CREATE TABLE prodlog (log_date DATE, p_code VARCHAR2(6));
```

When the trigger is fired the PL/SQL program (which consists of an INSERT statement only) is executed before (as we use of the BEFORE clause on the create statement), a row with one column, the current date is added into the prodlog table.

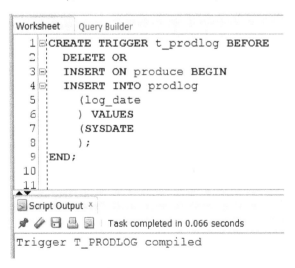

Example 14-9 Creating trigger

Conditioning the Trigger

You can add a condition restricting when a trigger should fire. The trigger in Example 14-10 has a condition using the FOR EACH ROW WHEN clause. Now, only if the new unit price (that is the unit_price after the update, thanks to the NEW reserve word) is higher than 2.00 the insert will be executed.

```
Worksheet    Query Builder
1 CREATE TRIGGER tcc_prodlog_when AFTER
2   UPDATE ON produce FOR EACH ROW WHEN (NEW.price > 2.00) BEGIN
3   INSERT INTO prodlog
4      (log_date
5      ) VALUES
6      (SYSDATE
7      );
8 END;
9
```

```
Script Output ×
       Task completed in 0.031 seconds
Trigger TCC_PRODLOG_WHEN compiled
```

Example 14-10 Trigger with condition

On top of the WHEN condition, you can further restrict by specifying specific columns on the UPDATE clause. The trigger created by Example 14-11 will only fire when the update is on the price column.

```
Worksheet    Query Builder
1 CREATE TRIGGER tc_prodlog_when AFTER
2   UPDATE OF price ON produce FOR EACH ROW WHEN (NEW.price > 2.00) BEGIN
3   INSERT INTO prodlog
4      (log_date
5      ) VALUES
6      (SYSDATE
7      );
8 END;
9
```

```
Script Output ×
       Task completed in 0.113 seconds
Trigger TC_PRODLOG_WHEN compiled
```

Example 14-11 Update on PRICE column

132

A trigger can also called stored procedures. Example 14-12 is an example trigger that calls a stored procedure, the increase_price that we created earlier.

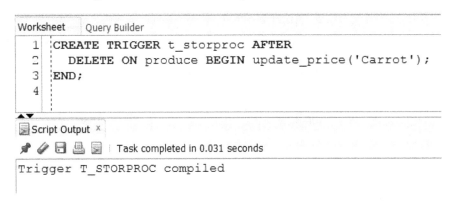

Example 14-12 Trigger calling stored procedure

Appendix A: Setting Up

This first chapter is a guide to install and set up the Oracle Database 11g Expression Edition release 2 and SQL Developer version 4. Both are available at the Oracle website for download at no charge.

Installing Database Express Edition

Go to http://www.oracle.com/technetwork/indexes/downloads/index.html

Locate and download the Windows version of the Oracle Database Express Edition (XE). You will be requested to accept the license agreement. If you don't have one, create an account; it's free.

Unzip the downloaded file to a folder in your local drive, and then, double-click the setup.exe file.

You will see the Welcome window.

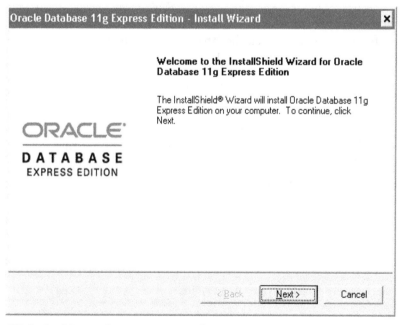

Click the Next> button, accept the agreement on the License Agreement window, and then click the Next> button again.

The next window is the "Choose Destination Location" window.

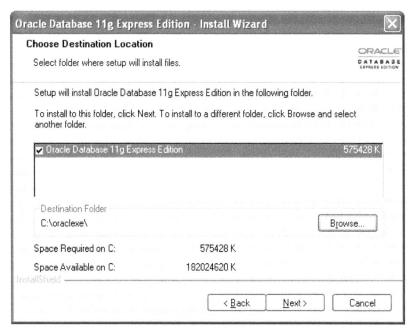

Accept the destination folder shown, or click the Browse button to choose a different folder for your installation, and then click the Next> button.

On the prompt for port numbers, accept the defaults, and then click the Next> button.

On the Passwords window, enter a password of your choice and confirm it, and then click the Next> button. The SYS and SYSTEM accounts created during this installation are for the database operation and administration, respectively. Note the password; you will use the SYSTEM account and its password for creating your own account, which you use for trying the examples.

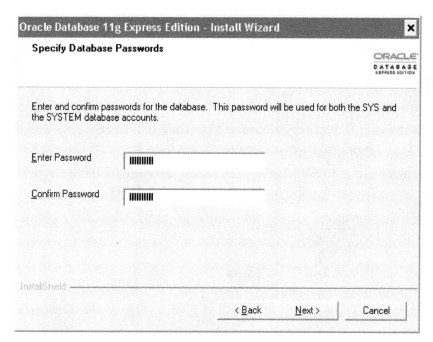

The Summary window will be displayed. Click Install.

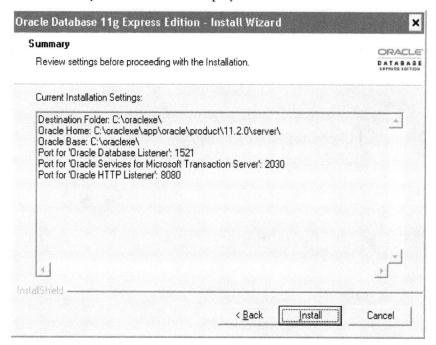

Finally, when the Installation Completion window appears, click the Finish button.

Your Oracle Database XE is now installed.

Installing SQL Developer
Go to http://www.oracle.com/technetwork/indexes/downloads/index.html

Locate and download the SQL Developer. You will be requested to accept the license agreement. If you don't have one, create an account; it's free.

Unzip the downloaded file to a folder of your preference. Note the folder name and its location; you will need to know them to start your SQL Developer.

When the unzipping is completed, look for the sqldeveloper.exe file.

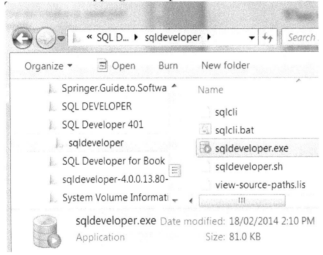

You start SQL Developer by opening (double-clicking) this file.

You might want to create a short-cut on your
Desktop.

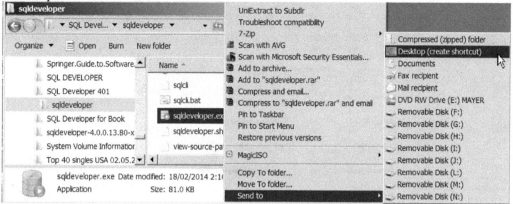

You can then start your SQL Developer by double-clicking the short-cut.

Your initial screen should look like the following. If you don't want to see the Start
Page tab the next time you start SQL Developer, un-check the *Show on Startup* box at
the bottom left side of the screen.

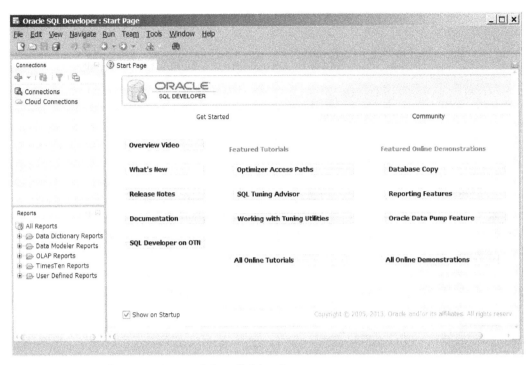

For now, close the Start Page tab by clicking its x.

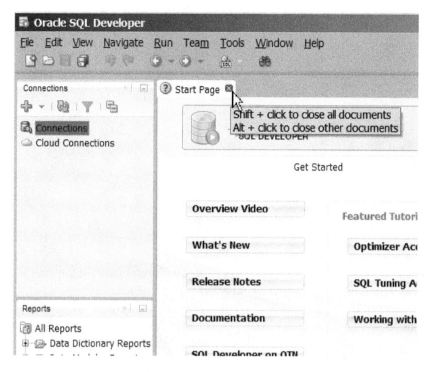

Creating Connection

To work with a database from SQL Developer, you need to have a connection.

A connection is specific to an account. As we will use the SYSTEM account to create your own account, you first have to create a connection for the SYSTEM account.

To create a connection, right-click the Connection folder.

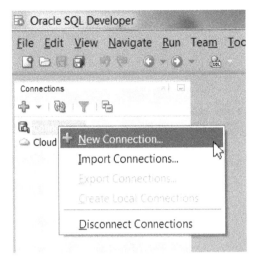

On the New/Select Database Connection window, enter a Connection Name and Username as shown. The Password is the password of SYSTEM account you entered during the Oracle database installation. Check the Save Password box.

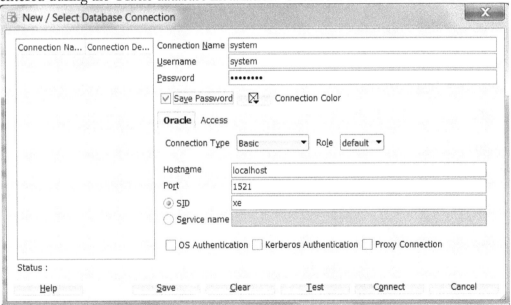

When you click the Connect button, the *system* connection you have just created should be available on the Connection Navigator.

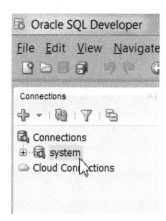

A Worksheet is opened for the system connection. The Worksheet is where you type in source codes.

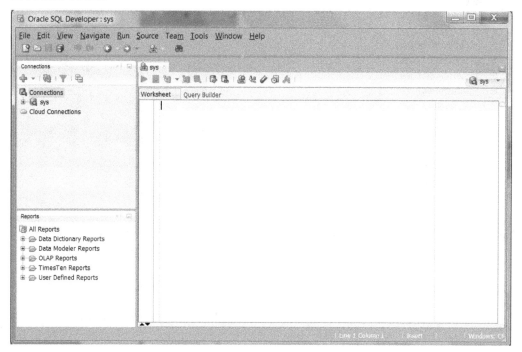

Creating Database Account

You will use your own database account (user) to try the book examples.

To create a new account, expand the system connection and locate the Other Users folder at the bottom of the folder tree.

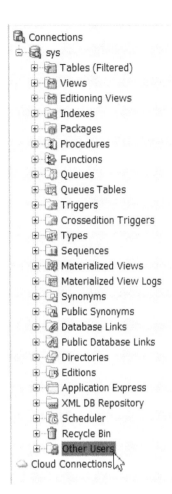

Right click and select Create User.

Enter a User Name of your choice, a password and its confirmation, and then click the Apply button. You should get a successful pop-up window; close it.

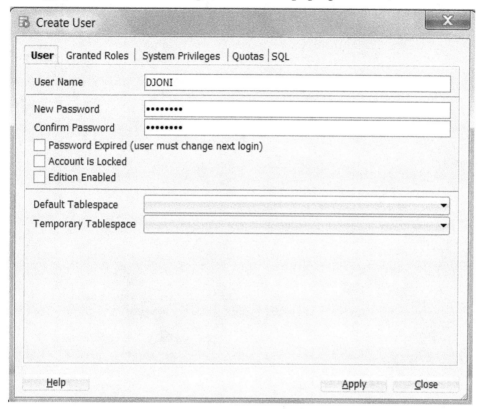

On the Granted Roles tab, click Grant All, Admin All and Default All buttons; then click the Apply button. Close the successful window and the Edit User as well.

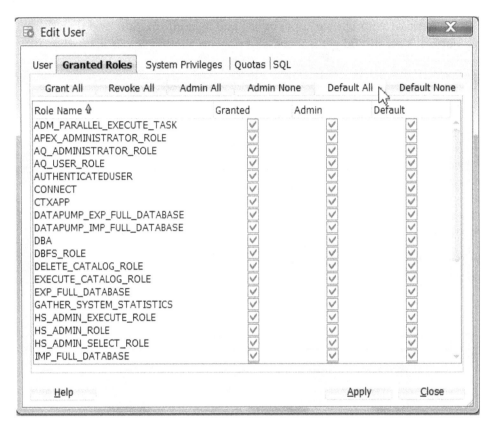

Creating Your Connection

Similar to when you created system connection earlier, now create a connection for your account.

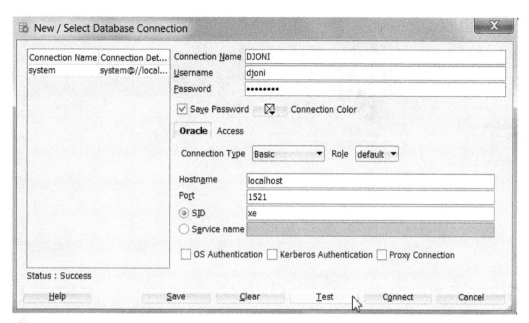

Click the Connect button. A worksheet for your connection is opened (which is *DJONI* in my case).

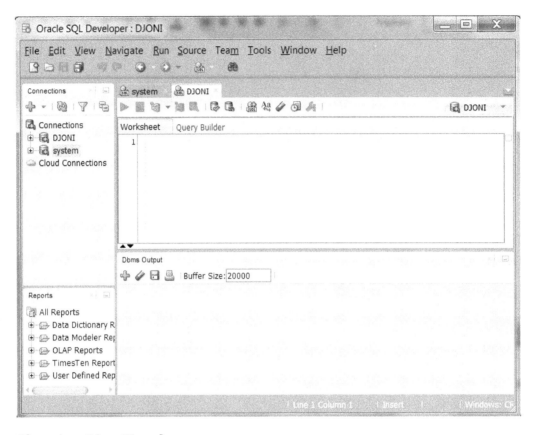

Showing Line Numbers

In describing the book examples I sometimes refer to the line numbers of the program; these are line numbers on the worksheet. To show line numbers, click Preferences from the Tools menu.

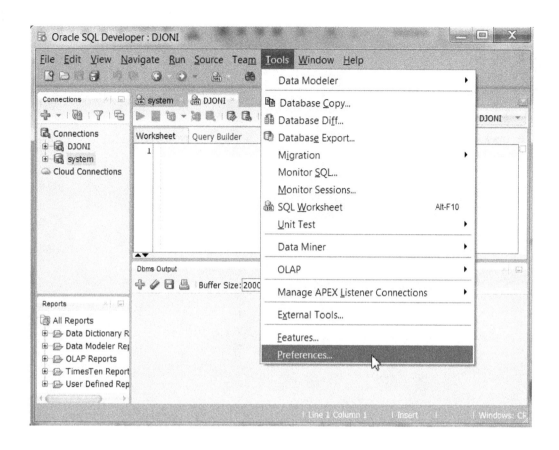

Select Line Gutter, then check the Show Line Numbers. Your Preferences should look like the following. Click the OK button.

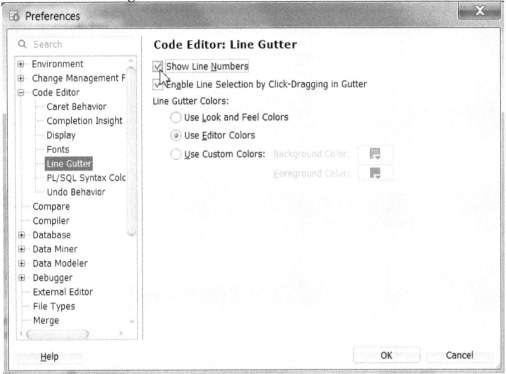

Deleting the *system* Connection

Delete the *system* connection, making sure you don't use this account mistakenly. Click Yes when you are prompted to confirm the deletion. Your SQL Developer is now set.

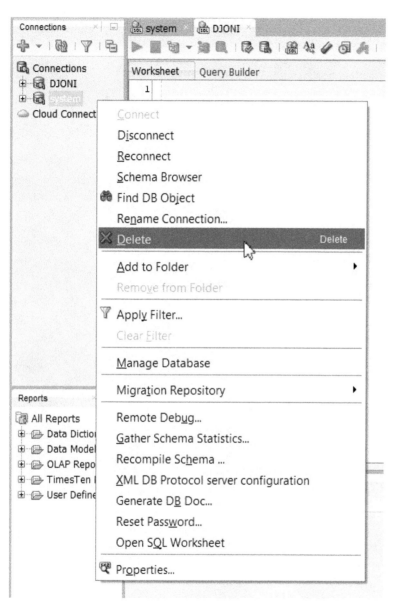

Close the *system* worksheet.

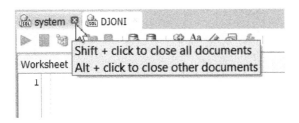

Appendix B: Using SQL Developer

This chapter shows you how to use the SQL Developer features that you will use to try the book examples.

Entering SQL statement and PL/SQL source code

The worksheet is where you enter SQL statement and PL/SQL source code.

Start your SQL Developer if you have not done so. To open a worksheet for your connection, click the + (folder expansion) or double-click the connection name. Alternatively, right-click the connection and click Connect.

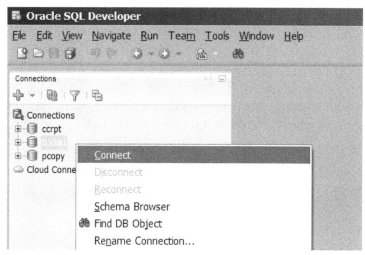

Note the name of the worksheet (tab label) is the name of your connection.

You can type source code on the worksheet.

Appendix A has the source code of all the book examples. Instead of typing, you can copy a source code and paste it on the worksheet.

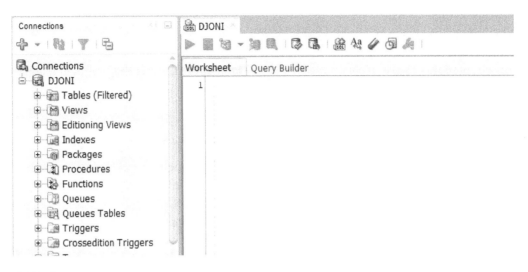

SQL Statement

Some of the book examples use a table named *produce*. Type in the SQL CREATE TABLE statement shown below to create the table (you might prefer to copy the *create_produce.sql* listing from Appendix A and paste it on your worksheet)

You run a SQL statement already in a worksheet by clicking the Run Statement button.

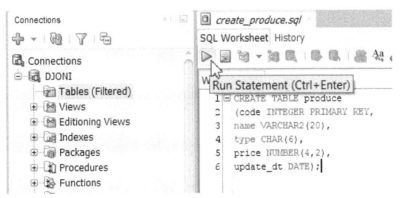

The Script Output pane confirms that the table has been created, and you should see the produce table in the Connection Navigator under your connection folder. If you don't see the newly created table, click Refresh.

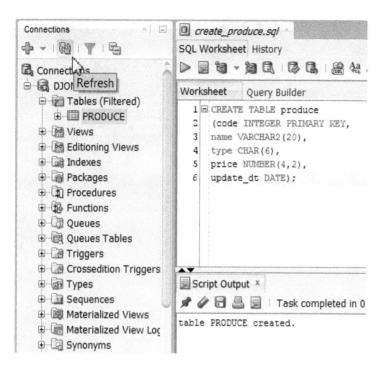

Inserting Rows

As an example of running multiple SQL statements in SQL Developer, the following five statements insert five rows into the produce table. Please type the statements, or copy it from *insert_produce.sql* in Appendix A. You will use these rows when you try the book examples.

Run all statements by clicking the Run Script button, or Ctrl+Enter (press and hold Ctrl button then click Enter button)

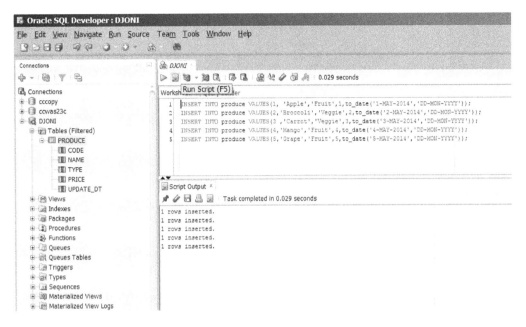

PL/SQL program

To learn how to run a PL/SQL program, type the following PL/SQL program, or copy it from *running_plsql.sql* in Appendix A.

You have not learned anything about PL/SQL programming yet, so don't worry what this program is all about.

To run the program, click the Run Script button or press F5.

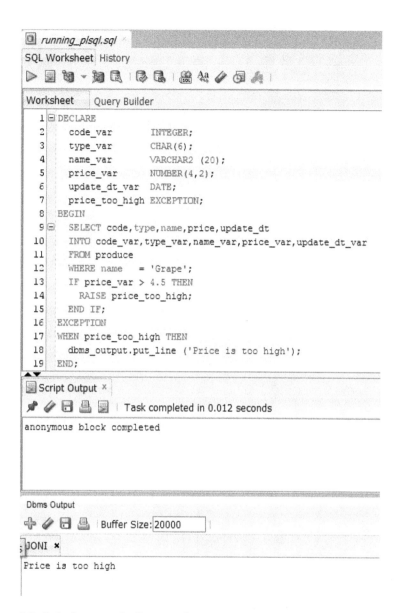

Multiple worksheets for a connection

Sometimes you need to have two or more programs on different worksheets. You can open more than one worksheet for a connection by right-clicking the connection and select Open SQL Worksheet.

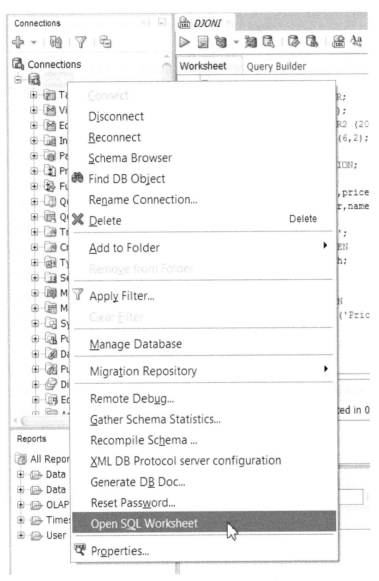

The names of the next tabs for a connection have sequential numbers added.

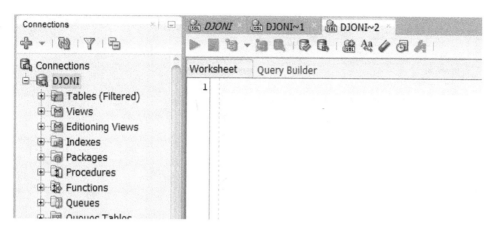

Storing the source code

You can store a source code into a text file for later re-opening by selecting Save from the File menu.

Select the location where you want to store the source code and give the file a name, and then click Save.

158

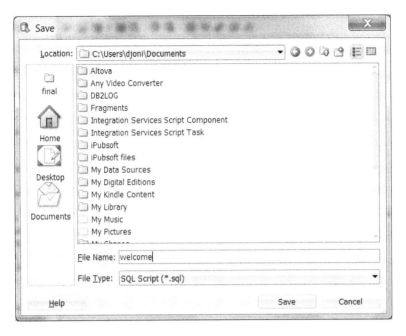

Opening a source code

You can open a source code by selecting Open or Reopen from the File menu and then select the file that contains the source code.

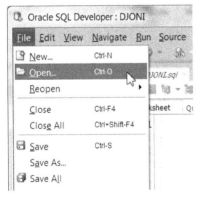

The source code will be opened on a new worksheet. The tab of the worksheet has the name of the file. The following is the worksheet opened for the source code stored as file named running_plsql.sql.

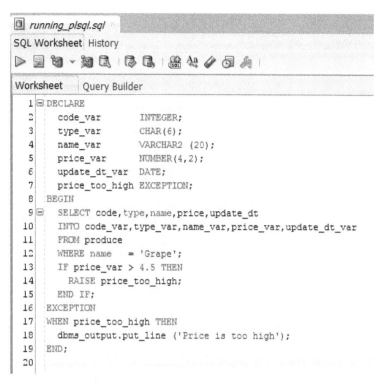

```
running_plsql.sql
SQL Worksheet  History

Worksheet      Query Builder
 1  DECLARE
 2      code_var        INTEGER;
 3      type_var        CHAR(6);
 4      name_var        VARCHAR2 (20);
 5      price_var       NUMBER(4,2);
 6      update_dt_var   DATE;
 7      price_too_high  EXCEPTION;
 8  BEGIN
 9      SELECT code,type,name,price,update_dt
10      INTO code_var,type_var,name_var,price_var,update_dt_var
11      FROM produce
12      WHERE name   = 'Grape';
13      IF price_var > 4.5 THEN
14        RAISE price_too_high;
15      END IF;
16  EXCEPTION
17  WHEN price_too_high THEN
18      dbms_output.put_line ('Price is too high');
19  END;
20
```

Storing the listings in Appendix A into files

As an alternative to copy and paste, you can store each of the listing into a file and then you can open the file. Note that you must store each program source code into a file.

Running SQL or PL/SQL from a file

You can execute a file that contains SQL statement or PL/SQL program without opening it on the worksheet as shown here.

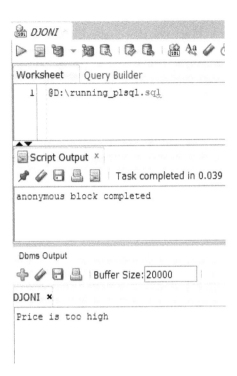

Clearing a Worksheet

To clear a Worksheet, click its Clear button.

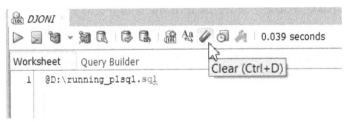

Displaying Output

Most of the book examples use the Oracle-supplied dbms_output.put_line procedure to display some outputs. For the book readers learning PL/SQL, the displayed output gives an instant feedback of what happens in the running program. Real-life programs might not need to display any output.

The dbms_output.put_line procedure has the following syntax.

```
dbms_output.put_line (parameter);
```

The value of the parameter must evaluate to a string literal (value).

When the procedure is executed in SQL Developer, the string literal is displayed on the Dbms Output.

To see the output, before you run the example, make sure you already have a Dbms Output pane opened for the connection you use to run the program. If your Dbms Output is not ready, set it up as follows:

Assume you want to run the program as shown here.

Click the View menu.

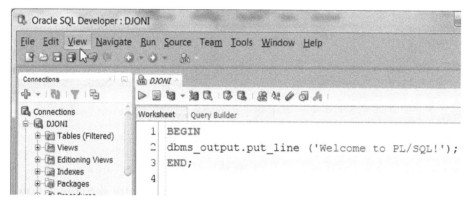

Next, select Dbms Output.

The Dbms Output pane is now opened.

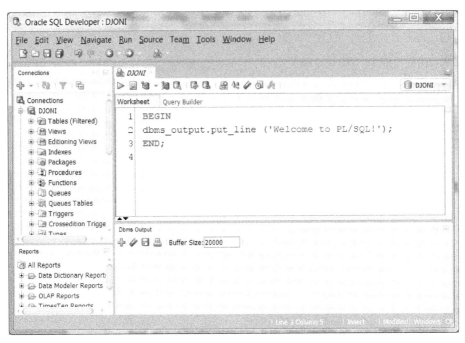

To display an output, you need to set up the Dbms Output pane for the connection you use to run the program. Click the + button on the Dbms Output pane.

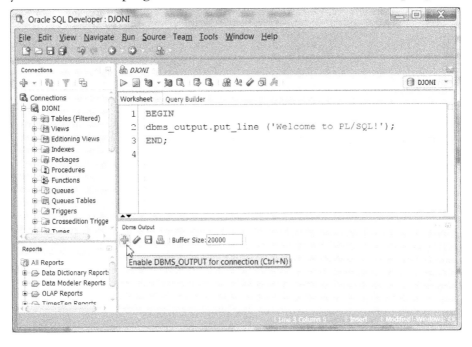

On the pop-up window, select the connection, and then click OK. As an example I select DJONI connection as this is the connection I want to use for running my PL/SQL program.

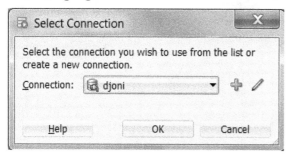

The Dbms Output now has the tab for the DJONI connection.

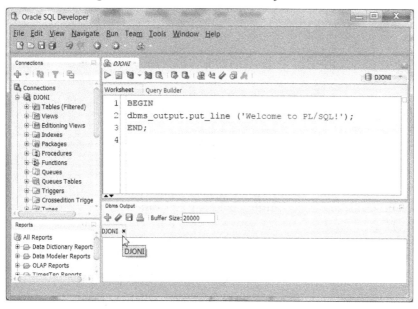

Now, run the program by clicking the Run Statement button. The Dbms Output pane displays the "Welcome to PL/SQL!" greeting. The message on the Script Output pane shows the result of running the program; in this case it indicates that the program is completed successfully. It would show an error message if the program is having a problem.

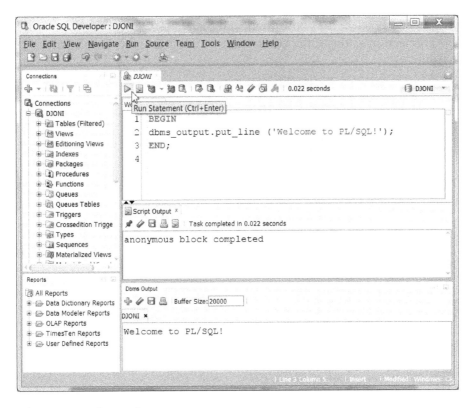

Clearing Dbms Output

To see a display output from a program, you might want to erase the output from a previous program. To clear a Dbms Output, click its Clear button.

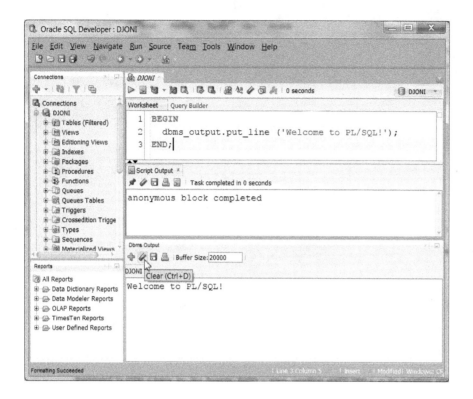

Index

A

Adding Rows · 6
Aggregate Functions · 22
Altering Table · 12

B

Block · 62
    Declaration Part · 62
    Exception-handling · 65
    Executable Part · 64
    label · 68
    multiple · 67
    nesting in Executable part · 67
    reserved words · 62
    structure · 62
Book examples
    creating table · 156
    inserting rows · 157
Built-in Function
    Character · 53
    Datetime · 55
    NULL-related · 57
    Numeric · 51

C

CASE · 23
    Searched CASE · 24
    Simple CASE · 23
Column Alias · 19
Comment
    multi-line · 72
    single-line · 72
Comparing to a List of Values · 17
Comparison Operators · 15
Compound Condition · 15
Compound Query

INTERSECT · 47
MINUS · 48
UNION · 46
UNION ALL · 45
Control statement · 82
    fixed iteration · 89
    IF THEN · 82
    IF THEN ELSE · 82
    IF THEN ELSIF · 85
    LOOP · 87
    Nested LOOP · 88
    Searched CASE · 93
    Simple CASE · 92
    WHILE loop · 90
Creating a Table · 5
Cursor · 117
    CLOSE · 117
    EXIT WHEN · 122
    FETCH · 117
    FOR LOOP · 123
    FOR LOOP short cut · 124
    last row · 120
    OPEN · 117
Cursor Attributes · 121
    %FOUND · 121
    %ISOPEN · 121
    %NOTFOUND · 121
    %ROWCOUNT · 121

D

Datatype · 75
    CHAR · 75
    DATE · 75
    INTEGER · 75
    NUMBER · 75
    ROWTYPE · 110
    TYPE · 110
    VARCHAR2 · 75
DDL (Data Definition Language) · 115
Deleting Data · 11
Displaying Output · 164

dbms_output.put_line procedure · 164
DISTINCT · 21

E

Exception-handling · 97
    combining exceptions · 98
    defining Oracle error · 102
    multiple statements · 98
    PRAGMA EXCEPTION_INIT · 102
    predefined exception · 101
    SQLCODE and SQLERRM functions · 102
    user defined exception · 103
    visibility · 99
Executable statement · 81
    assignment operator · 76
    Assignment, Computation, and Calling
        Procedure · 81

F

Filtering Rows · 14

G

Grouping
    GROUP BY · 31
    HAVING clause · 33
    Multiple Columns · 32

H

Handling NULL · 18

I

Imprecise Comparison · 18

J

Join
    More than Two Tables · 39
    Querying Multiple Tables · 37
    Table Aliases · 38

L

Limiting Number of Output Rows · 20

M

Multiple Transactions · 115

N

Negating Operator · 16

O

Oracle Database
    creating account · 145
    downloading · 137
    Express Edition (XE) · 137
    installing · 137
Ordering Output Rows · 26

P

Package
    Creating · 132
PL/SQL
    advantages over SQL's · 108

S

Savepoint · 114

SELECT statement · 13
SQL · 1
   Structured Query Language · 1
SQL Developer
   creating connection · 143
   downloading · 140
   installing · 140
   starting · 140
SQL Developer worksheet
   clearing · 164
   multiple worksheets · 159
   opening · 155
   opening a source code · 162
   running a PL/SQL program · 158
   running a SQL statement · 156
   showing source code line numbers · 150
   storing the source code · 161
Stored Programs
   Package · 132
Stored Programs · 130
Subprogram · 127
   calling function · 128
   calling procedure · 129
   function · 127
   procedure · 129
Subquery
   Correlated · 43
   Multiple-Row · 41
   Single-Row · 41

T

Transaction · 113
Trigger · 134
   Condition · 135

U

Updating Data · 10
Using SQL in PL/SQL · 108
   commit · 113
   DELETE · 113
   rollback · 113
   SELECT for UPDATE · 111
   SELECT with INTO clause · 109
   UPDATE · 108

V

Variable
   Constant · 79
   declaration · 75
   initial value · 76
   Initial Value · 76
   maximum length · 75
   name · 75
   NOT NULL · 78
   Same-Name · 71
   visibility · 69

www.ingramcontent.com/pod-product-compliance
Lightning Source LLC
Chambersburg PA
CBHW060135060326
40690CB00018B/3890